PAUL'S AEON THEOLOGY IN 1 CORINTHIANS

CENTRE FOR PENTECOSTAL THEOLOGY CLASSICS SERIES

PAUL'S AEON THEOLOGY IN 1 CORINTHIANS

CENTRE FOR PENTECOSTAL THEOLOGY CLASSICS SERIES

FRENCH L. ARRINGTON

CPT

CPT Press
Cleveland, Tennessee

Paul's Aeon Theology in 1 Corinthians
Centre for Pentecostal Theology Classics Series

Published by CPT Press
900 Walker ST NE
Cleveland, TN 37311
USA
email: cptpress@pentecostaltheology.org
website: www.cptpress.com

ISBN-13: 978-1-935931-92-8

Dedicated to my wife, Frances, who has constantly given her support and encouragement to me in my academic pursuits and who has patiently endured the burning of much midnight oil and managed to make a happy home for my children and me

and

to my daughter, Athena, and to my son, Lee, who have had to make sacrifices that this book might be completed.

CONTENTS

SERIES PREFACE

The Centre for Pentecostal Theology Classics Series makes available to a wider audience monograph length studies from previous generations that are of special significance for Pentecostal scholarship. While the works included are not all written by Pentecostal scholars, they all address themes and issues that inform constructive Pentecostal theology and/or make special contributions to such by means of methodology or approach.

PREFACE TO CPT PRESS EDITION

The early church focused on a variety of languages to express its message of hope. One of the ways the church spoke about the end times was the use of apocalyptic ideas and language. Biblical apocalyptic literature includes the books of Daniel and Revelation. As well as these two books, there are apocalyptic materials in the OT prophets (Zechariah, Isaiah 24-27, Ezekiel 37-39). In the NT, Jesus' discourse on the Mount of Olives (Matthew 24-25, Mark 13, Luke 21) is apocalyptic. Apocalyptic can be found also in other books outside of the Bible (2 Enoch, Jubilees, 4 Ezra, etc.).

Some of the major themes of apocalyptic are the hopeful expectation that lies in the future, the promise of salvation for the faithful and judgment for the wicked, God's sovereign power over the demonic powers of the temporal world, what will happen at the end of history, and the two ages ('This Age and the Coming Age'). As the title of this book suggests – *Paul's Aeon Theology in 1 Corinthians* – this study focuses on the apocalyptic idea of the two ages and is limited to the way the two ages can be viewed as the substructure of 1 Corinthians.

The Apostle Paul gave a different shape to the two ages. Most Jews of the first century CE understood that there was a gap of time between 'this age' and 'the coming age'. For Paul, the first coming of Christ into this world had modified the two-age scheme. The age to come is no longer completely in the future because it has broken into this age – in measure – by the death and the resurrection of Christ. So the coming age is no longer merely in the future. Aware of that, Paul teaches that that God's saving activity in Jesus has been ushered into this age, but the end will not fully come until Christ returns.

After the first coming of Christ, the coming age has penetrated the old age of sin and death and the two ages have overlapped. Therefore, we find in Paul's teaching what has been called 'the already-not yet'. The change in the two ages and their overlapping are the result of them being bound to faith in Jesus Christ.

As an aid to understanding the two-age motif in 1 Corinthians, we will briefly examine a number of scholars' views of apocalyptic and then review the prominent themes of apocalyptic. Hopefully this prepares the readers sufficiently for considering Paul's aeon theology in 1 Corinthians.

I must not forget to thank Dr. John Christopher Thomas and Dr. Lee Roy Martin, professors at the Pentecostal Theological Seminary, who are responsible for the editing and reprinting of this book.

French L. Arrington, PhD

Professor of New Testament Greek and Exegesis, and Niko Njotoraharjo Chair for the Restoration of the Tabernacle of David at Pentecostal Theological Seminary, Cleveland, TN USA

PREFACE TO FIRST EDITION

I wish to acknowledge my indebtedness to my dissertation committee. Dr Eugene S. Wehrli, of the faculty of Eden Theological Seminary, who has a keen interest in biblical apocalyptic, has been a constant encouragement and has offered most useful suggestions. Father Charles H. Miller, SM, of the faculty of St. Louis University, who kindled my interest in apocalyptic in his course, 'Biblical Apocalyptic', has been most helpful in sharing bibliographic information and in offering very valuable suggestions. The kindness and assistance of these two scholars will not be soon forgotten. I wish especially to thank Dr Keith F. Nickle, Chairman of the Department of Biblical Languages and Literature at St. Louis University, who has served as the chairman of this dissertation committee. He is due gratitude for many reasons. First, for allowing me to do independent study under his supervision that I might get better acquainted with how apocalyptic had been handled in Pauline research. Second, for his constant encouragement to me and for his willingness to answer queries I have raised with him. Third, for his thorough reading of each of the installments of the manuscript and for his many very helpful suggestions. My special thanks to Miss Peggy Jane Bell, executive secretary of the Graduate School of Christian Ministries, for her assistance in typing the final draft.

INTRODUCTION

The interpretation of hope in the New Testament focuses on the variety of eschatological language employed by the primitive Church to formulate its faith and *Weltanschauung*. Apocalyptic was one of the primitive Church's modes of conceptualizing. In contemporary New Testament interpretation apocalyptic is considered to be a historical and theological problem.[1] Investigation has shown that late Jewish apocalyptic motifs penetrated the New Testament.

A current question is just how much of an influence did apocalyptic thought have on New Testament writers and their conceptualization?[2] This investigation does not propose a full-scale inquiry of

---

[1] Robert W. Funk (ed.), *Apocalypticism* (Journal for Theology and the Church 6; New York: Herder and Herder, 1969), focuses on various facets of the present problem of apocalyptic in biblical studies, but see especially Funk's discussion of 'Apocalyptic as an Historical and Theological Problem in Current New Testament Scholarship', pp. 175-91.

[2] Ernst Käsemann has reopened the question of early Christian apocalyptic with his provocative assertion: 'Apocalyptic – since the preaching of Jesus cannot really be described as theology – was the mother of all Christian theology'. See 'The Beginnings of Christian Theology', in Robert W. Funk (ed.), *Apocalypticism* (Journal for Theology and the Church 6; New York: Herder and Herder, 1969), p. 40. The essay was first published in German: 'Die Anfänge christlicher Theologie', *Zeitschrift für Theologie und Kirche* 57 (1960, 1962-85); and it appears also in Käsemann's *New Testament Questions of Today* (trans. W.J. Montague; Philadelphia: Fortress Press, 1969), pp. 82-107. Likewise, David N. Freedman, 'The Flowering of Apocalyptic', in Robert W. Funk (ed.), *Apocalypticism* (Journal for Theology and the Church 6; New York: Herder and Herder, 1969), p. 167, finds apocalyptic to be the controlling factor in the literature of the New Testament. He explains that 'the content and context of the Synoptic Gospels are inescapably apocalyptic, that the atmosphere in which the early church lived and its frame of reference were overwhelmingly apocalyptic, and that the rest of the New Testament writings to a greater or lesser extent reflect the same prevailing tone'. William A. Beardslee, too, is confident that apocalyptic is crucial to New Testament interpretation. 'Many of the central New Testament symbols', says Beardslee, 'for interpreting God's

the New Testament against the background of apocalyptic. Rather it is circumscribed to Paul's First Letter to the Corinthians.

The purpose of this study is to investigate the relation of Jewish apocalypticism, especially the apocalyptic scheme of the two-aeons, to Paul's First Letter to the Corinthians. After the problem and method of approach and the distinction between apocalyptic genre and theological motifs are stated, the study focuses on: (1) the thought of a number of scholars who see a correlation between Paul's thought and Jewish apocalypticism; (2) theological motifs of late Jewish apocalyptic; (3) the apocalyptic scheme of the two-aeons in 1 Corinthians; and (4) conclusions and implications.

To trace some of the contours of the past debate and to demonstrate that the functional significance of apocalyptic in Pauline thought is far from settled, the thought of a number of scholars is examined. Johannes Weiss was the first to demonstrate decisively that the message of primitive Christianity, including that of Paul, was couched in terms of Jewish apocalyptic. For Weiss, the thrust of Paul's eschatological message was that the new age has arrived and that the Christian already possesses the fulness of salvation. Likewise, Rudolf Bultmann and C.H. Dodd do not think that the apocalyptic element is fundamental to Paul's eschatology. According to

---

coming to man, including the resurrection, the kingdom of God and the Messiah or Christ are apocalyptic symbols'. See also his essay, 'New Testament Apocalyptic in Recent Interpretation', *Interpretation* 25 (1970), p. 419. It should be assumed, however, that most scholars are convinced that apocalypticism is the hermeneutical key to the New Testament. Both Gerhard Ebeling and Ernst Fuchs have reacted negatively to Käsemann. Their reactions are formulated in their essays in *Apocalypticism*, pp. 47-98. Ebeling concedes that the beginnings of Christianity are entwined with Jewish apocalyptic but that it is going entirely too far to say that the relation was that of parent to child, pp. 45-46. In his critique of Käsemann's position, Wayne G. Rollins, 'The New Testament and Apocalyptic', *New Testament Studies* 17 (1970-71), pp. 454-76, expresses the same opinion: 'None of the language systems called upon to "give voice" to the original event (the Christ-event) can properly be called the "mother of Christian theology",' p. 472. However, convinced that primitive Christianity was fundamentally apocalyptic in character, Helmut Koester, *Trajectories through Early Christianity* (Philadelphia: Fortress Press, 1971), p. 154, observes, 'He (Käsemann) is certainly right in his emphasis upon the tremendous importance of apocalyptic thought in the early years of Christianity; I would add: upon both Christian heresy and Christian orthodoxy'. Klaus Koch, *Ratlos vor der Apokalyptik* (Gütersloh: Gerd Mohn, 1970), too, insists that apocalyptic is an important but neglected area of biblical studies. The debate is far from settled. Anyway, one of the primitive church's modes of conceptualizing was supplied by Jewish apocalypticism.

Bultmann, once apocalyptic forms have been interpreted existentially, they are no further use in understanding the New Testament. Dodd maintains that Paul abandoned the apocalyptic *Weltanschauung* in his later letters. Both Bultmann and Dodd see the emphasis of Paul's theology as falling on individual salvation and the present inward participation of the Christian in the powers of the new age. In contrast, Albert Schweitzer and Ernst Käsemann contend that present eschatology is not the dominating center of Paul's thought but that cosmic and futuristic dimensions of apocalypticism are decisive to Paul's theology. In seeking the background of the distinctive eschatological ideas in 1 Corinthians, the raw material of late Jewish apocalyptic is reviewed with the stress falling on such motifs as the understanding of history (unity, dualism, and determinism), the *Urzeit-Endzeit* scheme, angelic and demonic powers, messianic expectation, and the final judgment. The survey reveals that apocalyptic is not a unified phenomenon. While the apocalyptists differ in details, the above motifs are characteristic of their writings.

The exegetical study of 1 Corinthians shows the interpenetration of late Jewish apocalyptic in 1 Corinthians. The entire perspective seems to be conditioned by Paul's belief in the two ages, but the Apostle modifies the Jewish apocalyptic scheme of the two ages by teaching that the new age dawned in the Christ-event; and, as a result, 'the age to come' penetrates 'this age'. The Pauline present is a time in which the ages overlap. Therefore, the study demonstrates that fundamental to 1 Corinthians is the dialectical relationship of 'this age' and 'the age to come'.

1

THE PROBLEM AND METHOD OF APPROACH

The purpose here is to state the question to which this study addresses itself and the methodological procedure that will be followed. Some of the sources used in this investigation will conform to apocalyptic in theological thought only but not in literary form. Consequently, included is a statement that makes a distinction between apocalyptic in the sense of literary characteristics and apocalyptic in the sense of theological ideas.

The Problem

This study examines Paul's First Letter to the Corinthians against the background of Jewish apocalyptic. The intention is not to consider all the nuances of Pauline eschatology nor will more than cursory consideration be given to problems in Pauline research that would lead away from our principal concern. Such problems include the following: (1) the integrity of 1 Corinthians,[1] (2) whether the opponents

---

[1] Its integrity has been questioned, but the evidence is not convincing. Cf. Werner G. Kümmel, *Introduction to the New Testament* (trans. A.J. Mattil, Jr.; New York: Abingdon Press, 1965), pp. 203-204. Walter Schmithals, *Gnosticism in Corinth: An Investigation of the Letters to the Corinthians* (trans. John E. Steely; New York: Abingdon Press, 1971), maintains that 1 and 2 Corinthians have no less than fragments of six letters of Paul to Corinth. Supposedly, these were put together by an editor who designed them as an anti-Gnostic polemic, and 1 Corinthians is made up of at least two pieces of two different letters. However, H.D. Wendland, *Die Briefe an die Korinther*, *Das Neue Testament Deutsch* (Göttingen Vandenhoeck & Ruprecht, 1955), VII, p. 4, proposes that in light of the fact that one cannot demonstrate that different situations are discernible throughout 1 Corinthians, the letter may be regarded as uniform (*einheitlich*). For a recent discussion of the problem in which the

of 2 Corinthians are different from those of 1 Corinthians, (3) the question of a shift in Paul's theology away from apocalyptic to Hellenistic thought-forms,[2] and (4) the problem of the continuing or declining importance of the *parousia* in Paul's theological stance.[3]

The purpose is not to investigate the origin[4] but the relation of Jewish apocalypticism – especially the apocalyptic scheme of the two-

---

integrity of 1 Corinthians is defended, see J.C. Hurd, Jr., *The Origin of 1 Corinthians* (New York: Seabury Press, 1965), pp. 43-47, 115-47.

[2] Paul's eschatological language did undergo change, but it was not a gradual development from Jewish into Hellenistic thought-forms. James M. Robinson and Helmut Koester, *Trajectories through Early Christianity*, propose that it is a dialectic relation, or a zig-zag course. William Baird, 'Pauline Eschatology in Hermeneutical Perspective', *New Testament Studies* 17 (1970-71), p. 327, observes:

> in the midst of the varieties of language, major eschatological concepts have remained relatively constant. Nevertheless, since theology and language are integrally related, change in language inevitably involves modification of meaning. This is particularly clear in Paul's reduction of apocalyptic language. Although apocalyptic elements appear in Romans and Philippians, the amount of apocalyptic has been reduced since the writing of I Thessalonians. Because apocalyptic language is used primarily to describe the indescribable future, the reduction of apocalyptic involves an increasing concern for the past and the present – a concern apparent even in Galatians (cf. v. 1-12; vi. 7-10) and II Cor. x-xiii (cf. x. 3-4; xi. 12-15).

[3] C.F.D. Moule, 'The Influence of Circumstances on the Use of Eschatological Terms', *Journal of Theological Studies* 15 (1964), pp. 1-15, claims that development of New Testament theology (eschatology) was conditioned more by what had happened, the incarnation, than flagging hopes because of the delay of the *parousia*.

[4] The following explanations demonstrate that the question of origin is far from settled: (1) Out of prophecy: See H.H. Rowley, *The Relevance of Apocalyptic* (London: Lutterworth Press, 1947); S.B. Frost, *Old Testament Apocalyptic* (London: Epworth Press, 1952); D.S. Russell, *The Method and Message of Jewish Apocalyptic* (Philadelphia: Westminster Press, 1964); Frank Moore Cross, 'New Directions in the Study of Apocalyptic', in Funk, Robert W. (ed.), *Apocalypticism* (Journal for Theology and the Church 6; New York: Herdor and Herder, 1969), pp. 157-65. Cross thinks that the primary source of Jewish apocalyptic was old Canaanite mystic lore, which is known to us from the Ugaritic texts, but that syncretistic elements should not be discounted in description of the evolution of apocalyptic. The apocalyptic doctrine of the two ages, which Cross finds in its beginnings in late exilic and early post-exilic literature, is fundamental to this study. Another who sees the roots of apocalyptic in Old Testament prophecy is Paul D. Hanson, 'Old Testament Apocalyptic Reexamined', *Interpretation* 25 (1971), pp. 454-78; 'Studies in the Origins of Jewish Apocalyptic' (PhD Dissertation, Harvard University, 1969). (2) Out of wisdom: Gerhard von Rad, *Old Testament Theology* (trans. D.M.G. Stalker; New York: Harper and Row, 1965), II, pp. 301-15, proposes that apocalyptic is a Gnostic, syncretistic out-growth of wisdom literature. Von Rad expands this in *Wisdom in Israel* (Nashville: Abingdon Press, 1972). Furthermore, Klaus Berger, 'Zu den sogenannten Satzen heilgen Rechtes', *New Testament Studies* 17 (1970), pp. 10-40, believes that apocalyptic grew out of wisdom thought and that it shifted the judgment more

aeons – to the eschatology of the First Letter to the Corinthians. The principal concern is the apocalyptic notion of 'this age' and 'the coming age' along with Paul's use of apocalyptic nomenclature and his reinterpretation of the world-view of Jewish apocalyptic eschatology in relating it to the Christ-event. One task is, therefore, to seek the starting point or background of the distinctive eschatological thought of 1 Corinthians.[5] A second is the detection of similarities of eschatological thought of 1 Corinthians with apocalyptic motifs current in Paul's day. A third task is the assessment of the modification to which they have been subjected and their ultimate meaning (*Sachkritik*) in this letter. Consequently, our basic problem is to show the interpenetration of late Jewish apocalyptic in 1 Corinthians and to clarify its significance in this letter.

The Method

The subject matter is treated in five chapters. In addition to stating the purpose and methodological procedure of this study, Chapter 1 seeks to explain that the essence of apocalyptic is not controlled by the literary genre.

Theological motifs found in Jewish apocalyptic appear in the Pauline *corpus*, but the literary form of Paul's letters does not conform to

---

and more into the hands of God. See especially pp. 22-24. (3) Within Hellenistic-Oriental syncretism: Hans D. Betz, 'On the Problem of the Religio-Historical Understanding of Apocalypticism', in Robert W. Funk (ed.), *Apocalypticism* (Journal for Theology and the Church 6; New York: Herder and Herder, 1969), pp. 137-38, sees apocalypticism as a phenomenon within the entire course of Hellenistic-Oriental syncretism. Cf. also Otto Ploeger, *Theokratie und Eschatologie* (Neukirchen: Neuenkirchener Verlag, 1959). In Chapter III, 'Erwägungen zum Aufkommen der Apokalyptik', Ploeger takes note that one of the differences between apocalyptic and prophecy is that the monistic eschatology of prophecy is foreign to apocalyptic eschatology, which is dualistic Iranian in origin. He finds that the postexilic community was trying to isolate itself from all foreign influences and to establish itself as a critically pure people. Paradoxically, it is just this concept of the cultic community which freed Israel of the dangers of a politically interpreted eschatology and allowed the suppressed feelings of the people to come to the surface. It was these eschatological hopes which Israel borrowed from foreign sources but which she reshaped in order to accommodate them to the basic concepts of the Jewish faith.

    [5] Cf. H. St. John Thackeray, *The Relation of St. Paul to Contemporary Jewish Thought* (New York: Macmillan Company, 1900), pp. 98-99. It is evident from Thackeray's study that Paul was dependent on apocalyptic traditions of Judaism. Especially does he compare the eschatological details of 1 and 2 Thessalonians and 1 Corinthians with relevant passages in apocalyptic and rabbinic literature.

the form and style of apocalyptic genre. In 1 Corinthians, apocalyptic vocabulary and motifs appear in literary sections which are not apocalyptic in form. The determination of the influence of apocalyptic conceptuality on Paul in 1 Corinthians makes important an articulation of the distinction between apocalyptic with reference to literary form and with reference to distinctive theological motifs.

Chapter 2 draws attention to scholarly assessment of apocalypticism in the New Testament. The intent is to bring into focus the problem of apocalyptic in the interpretation of the New Testament. This involves examining the works of a number of scholars of the past and present and assessing the role they have assigned to apocalypticism in interpreting the New Testament. Such an effort is designed not only to determine what prominence has been given to apocalyptic in New Testament scholarship in the past but also what the present state of the problem is, especially what importance and place are ascribed to apocalypticism in Paul's theology.

Chapter 3 brings together the themes that are common to Jewish apocalyptic. The aim of this analysis of the raw material, which in some instances is only in accord with apocalyptic in message but not in form (*Gattung*), is to construct the theology of Jewish apocalyptic so that traces and motifs of apocalypticism are exposed in 1 Corinthians. To grasp the prominence and the meaning of apocalyptic in Paul, it is not enough to trace the tradition to some presumed source or determine its theological framework. It is equally important to attempt to assess the meaning of the tradition in the context of the literary works of which it is part. At this point a methodological problem arises. There are extant apocalyptic sources that date from before the first century. Included in these are the Book of Daniel (165 BCE), 1 Enoch (from c. 164 BCE onwards), Jubilees (c. 150 BCE), Sibylline Oracles, Book III (from c. 150 BCE onwards), Testaments of the Twelve Patriarchs (latter part of second century BCE), and Psalms of Solomon (c. 48 BCE). However, a number of apocalyptic works are later than Paul's time. Examples are the Life of Adam and Eve (shortly before CE 70), Sibylline Oracles, Book IV (c. CE 80), 4 Ezra (c. CE 90), II Baruch (after CE 90), 3 Baruch (second century CE), and Sibylline Oracles, Book V (second century CE).[6] Should

---

[6] The dates follow the dating of apocalyptic writings by Russell, *The Method and Message of Jewish Apocalyptic*, pp. 37-38.

apocalyptic sources that are available but dated later than the first century be considered in assessing apocalyptic as a factor in I Corinthians? It should be kept in mind that works dated later preserve older traditions. A number of apocalyptic writings are thought to be composite in character and to contain material that comes from a period of several decades.[7]

It is almost impossible to trace dates of origin exactly. They can only be approximate. It could be that some of the documents are older than is generally thought. Anyway, because of the syncretistic nature of apocalyptic works, it is difficult to deny that they include older tradition. Therefore, while a few of the works cited in our study may be normally dated second century CE or later, it is possible that they reflect traditions that are first century or earlier. This study draws attention to apocalyptic materials, some of which are considered to antedate historically the Pauline Letters and others which are thought to postdate Paul's time.

Chapter 4 is an exegetical study[8] of significant passages of 1 Corinthians to determine the use of Jewish apocalypticism as one of the modes of Paul's conceptualizing and more particularly to explore the significance of the dialectical relationship of 'this age' and 'the age to come' in the letter. Use is made of some of the more recent scholarly suggestions along with my own insights.

The approach, however, is not that of looking for direct historical connections of apocalyptic with 1 Corinthians but rather the plotting of a cultural *Sitz im Leben* from which both sprang. It is necessary to fix the cultural milieu underlying both apocalyptic and 1 Corinthians on its trajectory and consider 1 Corinthians within the broad context of apocalyptic thought.[9] If the ideas of Paul and apocalyptic are seen as emanating from the same fundamental matrix, a comparison of

---

[7] See Russell, *The Method and Message of Jewish Apocalyptic*, pp. 58-59 for examples.

[8] The historical-grammatical-exegetical method is deemed valid.

[9] Robinson, *Trajectories through Early Christianity*, p. 3, observes,

The whole purpose in applying generalizations, in subjecting data to analysis and synthesis, to categorization, is to open, both the text and experience to broader and deeper understanding to a higher degree of intelligibility to significance beyond particulars. Such generalization is not basically the addition of something extraneous to the data but rather the detection, through rigorous methodical observation, of specific additional data, namely the interrelatedness within the data, the ways in which they cohere. Boundaries between categories, the contours and directions they indicate, are assumed to apply in some way to the reality being studied.

the two should draw attention to the distinctive dissimilarities as well as similarities. Without postulating any direct historical connection, we can explain the similarities by the fact that both shared a common milieu.

This raises a question about methodological procedure. Scholars have increasingly recognized that the first-century milieu against which we place Paul was variegated and highly complex. In the light of the multiple intricacy of Paul's background and the fact that there were other forces in addition to apocalypticism at work in shaping his thought,[10] why confine ourselves to detecting apocalyptic influences and affinities in 1 Corinthians? It is believed that the apocalyptic doctrine of the two-aeons is more fundamental to Pauline thought, especially in 1 Corinthians, than has been generally recognized by modern biblical scholarship. From the standpoint of his Jewish heritage (Phil. 3.5; Rom. 11.1; 2 Cor. 11.22; Gal. 1.14) the intellectual and religious forces of late Judaism exercised a strong influence on Paul.[11] To some extent at least his apocalyptic beliefs prior to conversion must have coincided with his Christian beliefs.[12]

---

[10] It is an over-simplification to categorize Paul as an apocalyptic theologian. Betz, 'The Concept of Apocalyptic in the Theology of the Pannenberg Group', in Robert W. Funk (ed.), *Apocalypticism* (Journal for Theology and the Church 6; New York: Herder and Herder, 1969), p. 205, asserts, '… Paul's religio-historical conceptuality is much too complex to be called simply "apocalyptic"'.

[11] Modern scholars have attempted to approach Paul from a number of angles: The Old Testament, Hellenism, Hellenistic Judaism, Rabbinic Judaism, and apocalyptic. Each of these have contributed something to the understanding of Paul. It has been increasingly recognized that the first-century milieu against which we are to locate Paul was highly syncretistic and that a sharp dichotomy between Judaism and Hellenism in the first-century world is no longer tenable. See C.K. Barrett, *The New Testament Background* (New York: Harper and Row, 1956); W.D. Davies, *Paul and Rabbinic Judaism* (New York: Harper and Row, 1948); Victor R. Furnish, *Theology and Ethics in Paul* (New York: Abingdon Press, 1968), pp. 25-67.

[12] Luke describes Paul as a Pharisee in his early life (Acts 23.6; 26.5). Paul confirms it in Phil. 3.5. This raises the difficult question of the relation between Pharisaism and apocalypticism. Opinion is varied. George F. Moore, *Judaism in the First Centuries of the Christian Era* (3 vols.; Cambridge: Harvard University Press, 1927-30), I, p. 127, argues that since Rabbinic Judaism never recognized apocalyptic literature as authoritative, it is '… a fallacy of method for the historian to make them (the apocalypses) a primary source for the eschatology of Judaism'. Those who see apocalyptic as part of mainstream Judaism have dealt with the difficulty created by the rejection of apocalyptic from the Jewish Canon

with the contentions that Judaism after A.D. 70 became far more unified than it was previously and that literature which might well have played a marked part before A.D. 70 after that date lost its prestige; hence the exclusion of

Consequently, the problem here is to identify the conceptualization of apocalyptic theology that appears in 1 Corinthians and assess the significance of its function in the context of this letter.

Finally, in chapter 5, attempt is made to state the theological conclusions that issue from our research and study and to show the implications that the conclusions of this study may have for the investigation of other Pauline literature.

The argument of this work, therefore, is that Pauline eschatology[13] provides the fundamental perspective within which everything else is viewed. The eschatological emphasis of 1.7, 8 is the underlying motif of the entire letter of 1 Corinthians, specifically 3.10-17 and 4.1-5, reaching its climax in chapter 15. The entire perspective is conditioned by Paul's belief in the two-aeon scheme found in apocalyptic. The Apostle, however, gives a different shape to the apocalyptic

---

apocalyptic literature reflects not so much conditions in the time of Jesus as the disillusions with and reaction against apocalyptic speculation after A.D. 70.

W.D. Davies, *Christian Origins and Judaism* (Philadelphia: Westminster Press, 1962), pp. 25-26. Cf. Russell, *The Method and Message of Jewish Apocalyptic*, pp. 23, 27; and R.H. Charles, *The Apocrypha and Pseudepigrapha of the Old Testament* (2 vols.; Oxford: The Clarendon Press, 1913), II, p. vii.

[13] Eschatology is an ambiguous term. In the traditional sense it refers to the end and the pattern of events that include the *parousia* of the Lord, the general resurrection and judgment, the vindication and glorification of the faithful and the Kingdom of God. The word *eschatology* is used also in a more general sense: all that pertains to God's act of salvation and faith in that event are eschatological. Rudolf Bultmann, *Theology of the New Testament* (trans. Kendrick Grobel; New York: Charles Scribner's Sons, 1951), pp. 292-353, maintains that the Pauline idea of God's act of redemption in Christ marks the end of the powers of the old aeon and inaugurates the believer into a new aeon and into freedom from the law, sin and death. In this sense eschatology pertains to all temporal categories of the past, present, and future and to the believer who lives in the period where the new age overlaps the old age. That is, the believer lives at the junction of the ages where the power of the law, sin, and death oppose the power of the Spirit, righteousness, and life. Consequently, believers find themselves under the dominion of the Spirit and Life without being wholly free of sin and death. According to 1 Cor. 15.20-23, eschatology in its biblical formulation dates from the resurrection of Christ. Through the resurrection of Christ, the eschatological process has been set in motion. The *last things* are no longer merely future; they are present, actual realities. Hence as Jeremias has suggested eschatology can more appropriately be described as 'eschatology in process of realization' (sich realisierende Eschatologie). Cf. H.P. Owens, 'Eschatology and Ethics in the New Testament', *Scottish Journal of Theology* 15 (1972), p. 370. Since eschatology pervades Paul's thought and since the discussion of any Pauline teaching about Christ involves eschatology in the broad sense, our examination of 1 Corinthians will, however, include the eschatological thought of that letter in both senses and will keep in view the dialectic of 'already' – 'not yet'.

expectation. A new and final reality had broken in with the death and resurrection of Jesus, forcing him to modify the radical dualistic view of history found in apocalyptic Judaism. His focus is more on the moral and spiritual differences between the two ages than on a dualistic temporal distinction common in much apocalyptic theology.

The methodology that makes eschatology central to Pauline thought is not without its problems. D.E.H. Whitely observes that the apostle's theology is so 'closely integrated' that it seems tenable to center it on almost any one of the doctrinal motifs.[14] Gunther Bornkamm also recognizes that the themes of Paul's thinking interpenetrate one another. He goes on to insist that eschatology is fundamental to Paul's whole theology:

> ... without it (eschatology) the rest is inconceivable, his teaching on the Law, his doctrine of justification and salvation, and all else he has to say on the word of the cross, on baptism and the Lord's Supper, on the working of the Spirit and the nature of the church.[15]

Understanding, therefore, eschatology in the broader sense, we shall see that the texts and motifs examined in 1 Corinthians implicitly or explicitly include a correlation between 'this age' and 'the coming age'. The eschatological perspective is more discernible in some of the thoughts and themes of 1 Corinthians than in others, but the major themes as well as the coherence of Paul's gospel are deeply influenced by his understanding that Christian existence is eschatological.[16]

III. Apocalyptic: Genre and Theological Motifs

Scholarly opinion on the subject of what constitutes *apocalyptic* is widely divergent.[17] To enter the heated debate would not serve our

---

[14] D.E.H. Whitely, *The Theology of St. Paul* (Philadelphia: Fortress Press, 1972), p. xiv.

[15] Gunther Bornkamm, *Paul* (trans. D.M.G. Stalker; New York: Harper and Row, 1969), p. 197.

[16] Furnish, *Theology and Ethics in Paul*, p. 114, says, '... the heuristic key to Pauline theology as a whole, the point in which major themes are rooted and to which they ultimately are oriented, is the apostle's eschatological perspective'.

[17] *Apocalyptic* is derived from the ἀποκάλυψις, which means 'uncovering' or 'revelation'. *Apocalyptic* is ambiguous because there is no agreed list of apocalyptic

purpose. Important, however, here is the fact that the concept *apocalyptic* encompasses both a literary and a theological phenomenon and that apocalyptic form (*Gattung*) and message are not inevitably wedded to one another. This distinction is crucial to our study since some of the raw material which we intend to examine to determine the representative teaching and motifs found in apocalyptic conforms only to the message, not to the literary form. Likewise, Pauline epistles are not identified with the literary form of apocalypse, but certain terminology and motifs of Jewish apocalyptic are prominent in Pauline eschatology.[18]

Cognizant that the message of apocalyptic is found apart from the genre, Ebeling rightly deems it necessary 'to distinguish between apocalyptic in the sense of literary form known as *apocalypse* and apocalyptic in the sense of specific theological motifs'.[19] Although it is inaccurate to assume that Jewish apocalypses are homogeneous phenomena, in general certain literary features identify this literature and include visions, pseudonymity, messianic figure, angelology, demonology, numerology, predicted woes, astral influences, and animal symbolism.[20]

Fundamental to the phenomenon of apocalyptic is its eschatological message.[21] Prominent themes in the message are: (1) the doctrine of two-ages/two-aeons; (2) determinism and the imminent expectation of the end; and (3) universalism. As we had noted, the term *apocalyptic* may be applied to books (Daniel, Apocalypses of Baruch, etc.) because of their stylistic features; but the theology of apocalyptic may

---

books and no consensus on an exact definition of the term. Cross, 'New Directions in the Study of Apocalyptic', observes that his description of apocalyptic ten years ago sounds archaic to his ears today. In the same publication, Betz, 'On the Problem of the Religio-Historical Understanding of Apocalypticism', p. 135, warns that 'We must be clear about the fact that thus far we have stated only formal characteristics and that we have by no means as yet grasped the nature or the concept of apocalypticism itself'. See also Rollins, 'The New Testament Apocalyptic in Recent Interpretation', p. 535.

[18] In the Pauline Corpus 1 Thess. 4.13-18; 2 Thess. 2.1-12 and 1 Cor. 15.35-58 are the closest to Jewish apocalyptic literature.

[19] Ebeling, 'The Ground of Christian Theology', p. 52.

[20] Cf. Rowley, *The Relevance of Apocalyptic*, pp. 106-65, who maintains that the term *apocalyptic* designates a type of literature in which the secondary characteristics are common.

[21] Edgar Hennecke, *New Testament Apocrypha* (ed. Wilhelm Schneemelcher; English translation ed. R. McL. Wilson; Philadelphia: Westminster Press, 1964), II, p. 587.

be found apart from the characteristics of the genre (pseudonymity, use of visions, cryptic numbers, etc.). For example, many of the theological motifs of apocalyptic appear in the writings of a number of the canonical prophets. In keeping with the message of apocalyptic Joel speaks of the universal outpouring of the spirit of prophecy (2.28, 29), the cataclysmic changes of sun, moon, and earth (2.30-32), and the gathering of the nations in the valley of Jehoshaphat for judgment (3.2, 12). Conspicuously present in Isaiah are the characteristic apocalyptic motifs of universal judgment (24.1-2), the eschatological banquet (25.6-8), and the resurrection of the dead (26.19). Zechariah 9-14 shows the apocalyptic concern with the woes and distresses that usher in the final age and with the establishment of the final rule of God.

The literary form of apocalyptic was well-known at Qumran, both in Daniel and Enoch, but apocalyptic theologoumena permeate other literary forms which were discovered near the Dead Sea. The Hymns describe graphically the *pangs* which will come upon Israel, upon humankind and upon all of creation when God brings his kingdom (1QH 3). In the Commentary on Habakkuk appear such motifs as the judgment of the nations by the elect (1.12, 13a), the expectation of the imminent end of the world (2.1, 2; 2.1-11; 2.18), and determinism (2.36). Furthermore, in the Community Rule appear such motifs as a *determined end*, renewal of the World and rewards – the elect would inherit the 'glory of Adam' (1QS 4).[22]

Although what is understood by apocalyptic is undecided, there is no question of limiting it to what is identified as the literary *Gattung* of the apocalypses. Betz claims that *apocalyptic* applies to:

> First, a certain body of writings, the apocalypses, that is, revelatory writings which intend to reveal secrets of the transcendental world and the end-time; second, it applies to the world of concepts and ideas which comes to expression in those texts.[23]

Then in general *apocalyptic* denotes ideas and concepts which are common to this kind of literature. Our investigation includes the sections of a number of literary works with strong eschatological

---

22 *The Dead Sea Scrolls* (trans. Geza Vermes; New Heritage Press, 1962), will be used for citations unless otherwise specified.
23 Betz, 'On the Problem of the Religio-Historical Understanding of Apocalypticism', p. 135.

emphasis – Isaiah 24-27, Joel, Ezekiel 38, 39, Zechariah 9-14 and War Rule – which normally do not come within apocalyptic *Gattung* as well as a number that are apocalyptic in terms of the well-known theological and literary characteristics: I Enoch; Jubilees; Sibylline Oracles III, IV; Testaments of the Twelve Patriarchs; Psalms of Solomon; Assumption of Moses; Apocalypse of Abraham; 4 Ezra and 2 Baruch.[24] Rather than on the formal literary characteristics our primary interest is focused on the theological motifs.

---

[24] Our selection was made from the list of books which David S. Russell, *The Method and Message of Jewish Apocalyptic*, pp. 37-38, classifies as apocalyptic literature and from the works which he does not consider to be apocalyptic according to form but have sections that reflect the message of apocalyptic (Betz, 'On the Problem of the Religio-Historical Understanding of Apocalypticism', pp. 89-90).

2

APOCALYPTICISM IN RETROSPECT: SCHOLARLY OPINIONS

For the last seventy-five years the apocalyptic element in the New Testament has been a concern of New Testament investigation. Johannes Weiss, Albert Schweitzer, and more recently the discovery of the Dead Sea Scrolls are largely responsible for the renewed interest in how to interpret the New Testament in light of apocalyptic. Here our task is to trace some of the contours of the past debate and to demonstrate that the question of Pauline apocalyptic is far from settled. A history of Pauline interpretation is beyond our scope. Of interest to us are scholars who see a correlation between Pauline eschatology and Jewish apocalypticism, and views which have been significant in the discussion of Pauline eschatology. We shall study the works of Johannes Weiss, Albert Schweitzer, Rudolf Bultmann, C.H. Dodd, and Ernst Käsemann to assess how they proposed to handle apocalyptic in Paul's letters.

Johannes Weiss

The origins of the problem of apocalypticism in the interpretation of the New Testament lie primarily in the work of Johannes Weiss.[1]

---

[1] Johannes Weiss, *Die Predigt Jesu vom Reiche Gottes* (Göttingen: Vandenhoeck und Ruprecht, 1892). The English translation is *Jesus' Proclamation of the Kingdom of God* (trans. R.H. Hiers and D.L. Holland; ed. L.E. Keck; Lives of Jesus Series; Philadelphia: Fortress Press, 1971), pp. 9-10, 61-62, 84-85.

Weiss began with the *Religionsgeschichtlich Schule* presupposition that primitive Christianity and its origins must be viewed in terms of its background and environment as any other historical phenomenon. While Weiss insisted that 'origins' should be understood for the most part as a regrouping of older elements rather than in the sense of a new creation, he maintains that primitive Christianity took a special form namely the belief that the final era of the world had dawned and that the entrance of the future into the present was almost complete.[2] The special form is designated by Weiss as the dramatic element in primitive Christianity:

> This dramatic element in primitive Christianity, the tremendous rise of hope to an ultimate tension, the introduction of the future into the present which is already almost realized, the consciousness of the possession nearly almost certain of a redemption which the Jews believed to be still at an undetermined distance and about which the Gentiles who have no hope (I Timothy 4.13) and do not know, is the real subject which requires an elucidation.[3]

This leads Weiss to ask, 'How could the universal apocalyptic view held by the Jews be changed into a present eschatological consciousness?'[4] He finds that the fundamental eschatological orientation of primitive Christianity can be traced to Jesus, who, according to Weiss, understood the kingdom of God purely in terms of the apocalyptic expectations of the future.[5] Though the eschatology of the primitive church had its roots in Jesus' conception of the kingdom of God, Weiss detects a remarkable shift in emphasis from the future to the present.[6] This is indicated by the numerous appearances of the κύριος

---

[2] Johannes Weiss, 'Das Problem der Entstehung des Christentums', *Archiv für Religionswissenchaft* 16 (1913), pp. 425-26.

[3] Weiss, 'Das Problem der Entstehung des Christentums', p. 437.

[4] Weiss, 'Das Problem der Entstehung des Christentums', p. 437.

[5] Weiss, *Jesus' Proclamation of the Kingdom of God*, p. 82, states this succinctly: 'Indeed, one may say: Precisely from Jesus' own standpoint, his entire activity is not messianic, but of preparatory character. It is evident from a great number of passages that Jesus thinks the establishment of the βασιλεία τοῦ θεοῦ will be mediated solely by God's supernatural intervention.' Cf. Weiss, *Jesus' Proclamation of the Kingdom of God*, p. 129, where Weiss says that the messianic consciousness of Jesus as expressed in the title Son of Man reflects 'the thoroughly transcendental and apocalyptic character of Jesus' idea of the Kingdom of God'.

[6] The piety of primitive Christianity goes along in an eschatological rhythm. The disciples like all the Jews must also wait for the kingdom; but their hope has a different sound; the question, when does the kingdom come, was brought into a

with Χριστός, which signified not only the decline of the national factor but also the eschatological.

> The *parousia* of Christ remained important especially to the Jewish Christians. But for the majority of Gentile Christians there had now been granted a religion of the present which was against the prevailing eschatological religion of the early church.[7]

Weiss suggests that the essential features of this later religion with its apocalyptic hope and its emphasis on the present worship of the exalted κύριος, that is, the Christ cult, are pre-Pauline.[8] Here Weiss discerns a basic continuity between pre-Pauline Christianity and Pauline Christianity. While Paul maintains an eschatological orientation, he discovers that what Jesus expected in the future had already happened. As for the primitive church, so for Paul the temporal dualistic aspects of apocalyptic hope become secondary. The outcome was that Paul's stress fell on the presentness of salvation though he does at times speak of the incompleteness of the present condition and anticipate consummation.[9] The pervading theme in Paul's eschatology is that salvation is *already* complete with Christ.

That the messianic age has already begun is conceived by the apostle in terms of the doctrine of two ages, which Weiss designates as basic to Paul's thinking.[10] Weiss explains that

> generally with Paul *aeon* has wholly the meaning of *world*, and the antithesis between both ages or worlds is no longer simply considered temporally, but above all else quantitatively: 'this world' is that of the earth, the world of creation, or corruption, of sin;

---

stage somewhat shorter or longer, there can be no more doubt about the coming of the kingdom, for history has made a decisive step forward, the future is assured, for the chosen one has ascended on His throne, the rulership of the Messiah, i.e., the first period of the age of redemption (chiliasm) has begun. Indeed, the last and decisive battle against the principalities and powers opposing God's sovereignty is yet to come; but the mighty Victor is already here.

[7] Johannes Weiss, *Earliest Christianity* (ed. Fredrick C. Grant; 2 vols.; New York: Harper and Row, 1959), I, pp. 176-77. The original German is *Das Urchristentum* (Göttingen: Vandenhoeck und Ruprecht, 1914).

[8] Weiss thinks that the Christ cult had its beginnings among Jesus' own personal disciples. See 'Das Problem der Entstenhung des Christentums', pp. 334-35.

[9] Weiss, *Earliest Christianity*, II, p. 447.

[10] Weiss, *Earliest Christianity*, II, p. 603.

'that' world is the one pertaining to heaven, the world of everlasting life, of God.[11]

Because the Christians 'have already experienced the world to come within themselves (Heb. 6.4)',[12] Weiss is convinced that, though ideas of consummation are not completely absent from Paul, he has transcended the temporal dimensions of the apocalyptic scheme and the concept of 'age' as a cosmic epoch:

> … the Messianic age of Salvation has dawned (2 Cor. 6.2); … the end of the present age has come, and the new age has been inaugurated (1 Cor. 10.11) … His (Paul's) faith, also from now on, is an eschatological hope; he also belongs to those who wait for the reign of God (Mark 15.43) and hope to share therein (Gal. 5.21; 1 Cor. 6.10; 4.20; Rom. 14.17). Paul emphasizes very strongly at times the preliminary, the incomplete nature of the present conditions (Phil. 1.23; 1 Cor. 13.12); so securely is his life anchored in Heaven (Phil. 3.20); so vividly does he feel himself stranger here (2 Cor. 5.6), that occasionally the feeling of separation from Christ outweighs everything else. But these are passing moods; on the whole the feeling of joy prevails, that the Messiah has come and the fulness of the Messianic salvation with him.[13]

Essentially for Weiss Paul has broken through the apocalyptic temporal distinction of the two ages and the central Pauline concern is the new age that is within the Christian. Therefore, according to his view, the Pauline conception of the new age is in terms of one's religious status, that is, whether the human has experienced an inner change of direction or what Paul describes as a 'new creation'.[14]

Albert Schweitzer

Schweitzer set the stage for twentieth-century discussion of Pauline eschatology by calling attention to the apocalyptic nature of the apostle's eschatological thought. Following Weiss, he attempted to overcome the apocalyptic nature of primitive Christianity with his theory

---

[11] Weiss, *Earliest Christianity*, II, p. 604.
[12] Weiss, *Earliest Christianity*, II, p. 604.
[13] Weiss, *Earliest Christianity*, II, pp. 446-47.
[14] Weiss, *Earliest Christianity*, II, pp. 514-15.

of thoroughgoing eschatology.[15] According to Schweitzer it was perfectly clear that late Judaism, not Hellenism, was the soil out of which Paul's thought grew.[16] To use his own words:

> From his first letter to his last Paul's thought is uniformly dominated by the expectation of the immediate return of Jesus, of judgment and the Messianic glory.[17]

He goes on to maintain that the Pauline expectation that the end was at hand rested on the belief that the messianic era, that is, the new age was inaugurated with Jesus. This conviction led Paul to teach that salvation had already begun to come into operation.[18] Since the coming age penetrated the present age, the situation is that of the overlapping of the ages which he expected to continue until the *parousia*.

Schweitzer saw two motifs as normative for understanding Paul: (1) the believer's being ἐν Χριστῷ and (2) the universalistic eschatological expectation.[19] It is the latter motif that convinces Schweitzer that Paul's thought is consistently dominated by apocalypticism. However, a cursory examination of the ἐν Χριστῷ concept is vital to assessing Schweitzer's interpretation of apocalyptic categories in Paul.

---

[15] Cf. Werner G. Kummel, *The New Testament: The History of the Investigation of Its Problems* (New York: Abingdon Press, 1970), pp. 235-36. With the term 'eschatology' Schweitzer referred to what is known now as apocalypticism. Because of him the eschatological character of Jesus's teaching has been widely recognized. He chided many of his fellow theological craftsmen for being historical taxidermists, i.e., taking the apocalyptic innards out of Jesus and mounting him as a natural museum piece who embodied the great timeless religious truths. 'To put it more, prosaically,' claims Schweitzer, 'modern theology is at last about to become sincere'. *The Mystery of the Kingdom of God* (trans. W. Montgomery; London: A. & C. Black, 1925), p. 6.

[16] Albert Schweitzer, *Paul and His Interpreters* (trans. William Montgomery; New York: Schocken Books, 1964), p. 161.

[17] Albert Schweitzer, *The Mysticism of Paul the Apostle* (trans. William Montgomery; New York: Henry Holt and Company, 1941), p. 52. Elsewhere he asserts, 'The late-Jewish Messianic world-view is the crater from which burst forth the flame of the religion of eternal love'. *Out of Life and Thought* (New York: Rinehart and Winston, 1933), p. 69.

[18] Schweitzer, *The Mysticism of Paul the Apostle*, p. 52.

[19] E. Earle Ellis, *Paul and His Recent Interpreters* (Grand Rapids: Eerdmans, 1961), p. 25, notes, 'It was his great merit (1) that he (Schweitzer) sought to understand Paul's thought in terms of one fundamental concept, (2) that he recognized the central importance of eschatology and (Jewish) anthropology in the Apostle's doctrine of redemption, and (3) that he recognized the Holy Spirit and "en Christo" union as the realization of the New Age in the present'.

Schweitzer placed Christ-mysticism at the center of Paul's thought.[20] For him, the ἐν Χριστῷ formula expresses Paul's understanding of the new condition of the believers. By faith and baptism they begin to share in the death and the resurrection of Christ. As soon as they are 'in Christ', they belong to the messianic era.[21] The consequences of being-in-Christ are that in this present existence they are free from the law and sin,[22] and at the *parousia* the resurrection mode of their existence would be made manifest.[23] Thus, the interim between the resurrection and the *parousia* of Jesus is the time when the aeons overlap.[24] What remains to be disclosed at the *parousia* is simply the supernatural life that Christians already possess.[25]

As might be inferred, Schweitzer saw no essential discontinuity between the time before and after the *parousia*. His understanding was that when the end of the world did not come, the Apostle made an effort to deal with an immediate problem of the Christian faith: the temporal separation of the resurrection and the second advent of Jesus Christ.[26] The perspective was shifted by Paul's conception that the messianic age dawned with the resurrection of Jesus. Supposedly Paul gave the ἐν Χριστῷ formula its full eschatological content and this gave rise to what Schweitzer identifies as eschatological mysticism. Through a mystical union with Christ, Christians live already in the messianic era. Schweitzer is careful to note that Paul's mysticism is distinct from Greek and medieval mysticism and must be understood in the context of Jewish apocalyptic: 'It (Paul's mysticism) does not bring the worlds into contact in the mind of the individual man … but dovetails one into the other'.[27] Through Christ-mysticism the sensuous and the super-sensuous converge[28] and the Christians,

---

[20] Relating justification by faith to the periphery in Paul, he insists that the main crater of Pauline thought is 'the mystical doctrine of redemption through the being-in-Christ'. *The Mysticism of Paul the Apostle*, p. 225.

[21] Schweitzer, *The Mysticism of Paul the Apostle*, p. 142.

[22] Schweitzer, *The Mysticism of Paul the Apostle*, pp. 191-92 and p. 3, where Schweitzer writes, 'I am in Christ. In him I experience myself as a being who transcends this sensuous, sinful, and finite world and belongs already now to the transfigured world. In Him I am certain of my resurrection.'

[23] Schweitzer, *The Mysticism of Paul the Apostle*, p. 99.

[24] Schweitzer, *Paul and His Interpreters*, pp. 244-45.

[25] Schweitzer, *The Mysticism of Paul the Apostle*, p. 111.

[26] Schweitzer, *The Mysticism of Paul the Apostle*, p. 111.

[27] Schweitzer, *Paul and His Interpreters*, p. 242.

[28] Schweitzer, *Paul and His Interpreters*, p. 241.

belonging to both worlds, already here participate in the new age and live in the eternal while still in time.

However, Schweitzer understands that Paul retains a futuristic eschatology. The resurrection-life is received here by anticipation. Through Christ-mysticism Christians have moved into the messianic age, but the present existential dimension does not deplete the Pauline conception of the messianic age. Christians have not moved completely out of the old age. The messianic age *actually* begins after the *parousia*. According to Schweitzer the Apostle, without abandoning eschatological mysticism, expected an apocalyptic end.

Paul conceives of salvation, Schweitzer thinks, in apocalyptic dimensions of a world-event. He contends Pauline eschatology bears many affinities with the apocalypse of Baruch and Ezra. In particular, like both of the apocalypses, Paul does not equate the Kingdom of God with the messianic age.[29] Consequently Schweitzer maintains that the new age consists of two parts: the messianic era and the Kingdom of God. The messianic age *actually* begins after the *parousia* and only continues until the final victory of God. At the termination of the messianic age God becomes all in all.[30] So Schweitzer contends that Paul envisions something beyond the messianic age, namely cosmic salvation that includes man and the world. When the temporally limited messianic age gives way to the Kingdom of God, Christ-mysticism ceases and what Schweitzer calls God-mysticism begins. Faithful to the scheme of the apocalypses of Baruch and Ezra, Paul, according to Schweitzer, envisions that these are two successive epochs that are cosmic in scope. In light of his exposition it is clear that a decisive break exists between the two:

> Paul … does recognize a God-mysticism, but it is not in being contemporaneously with Christ-mysticism. The presuppositions of his world-view make it impossible that they should co-exist, or that one should necessitate the other. They are chronologically successive, Christ-mysticism holding the field until God-mysticism becomes possible.[31]

---

[29] Schweitzer, *The Mysticism of Paul the Apostle*, p. 88. Cf. *Paul and His Interpreters*, p. 50.
[30] Schweitzer, *Paul and His Interpreters*, p. 223.
[31] Schweitzer, *The Mysticism of Paul the Apostle*, p. 13.

Being-in-God, therefore, becomes a reality when angelic beings no longer possess any power over humans, and in the advancement of the messianic kingdom Christ has overcome them and death as the last enemy.[32]

What Schweitzer sees here is cosmic redemption. By faith and baptism the Christian enters into a 'new cosmic process'.[33] The renewal of the Christian that issues from participation in the death and resurrection of Christ and results in the natural state being replaced progressively by a supernatural one[34] is a world-process which Schweitzer argues has its beginning in the resurrection of Christ: 'Behind the apparently immobile outward show of the natural world, its transformation into the supernatural was in progress'.[35]

It must be made clear that for Schweitzer Paul envisions humanity as being caught up in two temporally successive cosmic-epochs: the temporary messianic era set into operation by Christ's resurrection and the eternal Kingdom of God. While the Christian participates in the messianic age by anticipation, Schweitzer disallows such participation in the final epoch. The Christian has passed from the old age into a new age, but not yet has he made his entrance into the final epoch of salvation. The passing of the individual into the final epoch is entrance into one that is distinct from the former one, i.e., even Christians who live in the messianic age by anticipation and after the *parousia* find themselves within the messianic age but have not entered the final state of blessedness – the Kingdom of God.

Obviously, Schweitzer understands that Paul envisions radical discontinuity between the messianic era and the Kingdom of God and that the decisive break occurs not at the *parousia* but after the *parousia* when the messianic age is displaced by the Kingdom of God. Then the present is not radically differentiated from the messianic age.

Sharp discontinuity does not exist between the period, before and after the *parousia*, but between the messianic age and the Kingdom of God. The messianic era which follows the *parousia* reaches its termination when Christ-mysticism gives way to God-mysticism and when it is displaced by the Kingdom of God.

---

[32] Schweitzer, *The Mysticism of Paul the Apostle*, pp. 12-13.

[33] Schweitzer, *Paul and His Interpreters*, p. 224.

[34] Schweitzer, *The Mysticism of Paul the Apostle*, p. 141. Cf. *Paul and His Interpreters*, p. 245.

[35] Schweitzer, *Paul and His Interpreters*, p. 99.

Rudolf Bultmann

Bultmann's approach, too, raises questions about the nature of Paul's eschatology. He does not think that apocalypticism was the dominant factor in the apostle's thought, as Schweitzer maintained, nor that Paul abandoned the apocalyptic *Weltanschauung* as we shall see that Dodd proposed. For him apocalyptic is an aspect of New Testament eschatology, and furthermore eschatology is not necessarily apocalyptic and should not be so understood in Paul, i.e. it does not fundamentally involve a cataclysmic end to history and the world but existence in the world 'as though not'.[36] But Bultmann observes that Paul retains the traditional eschatological expectation: 'To be sure, he (Paul) does not abandon the apocalyptic picture of the future, of the *parousia* of Christ, of the resurrection of the dead, of the Last Judgment, of the glory for those who believe and are justified'.[37]

While Bultmann does not think that Paul departed completely from his Jewish background, he does not find that apocalyptic elements are central to Paulinism. In fact, he sees Paul's modifying his historical perspective and reducing traditional eschatology to an anthropology.[38] (1) At first Paul's view of history was shaped by the Old Testament idea that history is divinely directed towards a goal. (2) Under the influence of the apocalyptic scheme of the two ages this was modified so that the Apostle interpreted history within the world-view of apocalyptic and the expectation that the end of the world would occur as the divine drama unfolded. The past was the uniform history of sin; the present is the intermediate messianic age – the time between the resurrection and the *parousia* of Christ. The new age has already dawned and will be fully disclosed by the imminent *parousia* of Christ. (3) Subsequently, the apocalyptic expectation

---

[36] Rudolf Bultmann, 'The New Testament and Mythology' in *Kerygma and Myth: a Theological Debate* (ed. H.E. Bartsch; trans. H. Fuller; New York: Harper and Row, 1961), pp. 5-6.

[37] Rudolf Bultmann, *The Presence of Eternity: History and Eschatology* (Edinburgh: The University Press, 1957), p. 42. Cf. Rudolf Bultmann, *Primitive Christianity in Contemporary Setting* (trans. R.H. Fuller; New York: World Publishing Company, 1956), pp. 198-99. *In his Theology of the New Testament*, I, p. 246, Bultmann maintains that Paul 'holds fast to the traditional Jewish-Christian teaching of the resurrection of the dead, and in so doing he also retains the apocalyptic expectation of the last judgment and of the cosmic drama which will end the old world and introduce the new world of salvation'.

[38] Bultmann, *Theology of the New Testament*, I, p. 191.

was modified by the influence of Gnosticism. As found in Gnostic thought, Paul essentially interpreted his present in terms of a dualistic understanding of humanity's existence. As the result of the non-appearance of the *parousia*, Paul demythologized apocalyptic and Gnostic concerns and historicized them so that they express humanity's understanding of themselves in the world.[39]

> In Jewish apocalyptic history is interpreted from the view of eschatology. In Paul history is swallowed up in eschatology. Thereby eschatology has wholly lost its sense as the goal of history and is in fact understood as the goal of the individual human being.[40]

It is clear to Bultmann that Paul abandoned his interest in temporal history for a personal historicity of the individual. No longer did the apostle have an interest in the history of Israel or the world; all of his concern is focused on the present-ness of Christian existence.[41] Accordingly Bultmann thinks the Apostle collapses the future dimension of his eschatology into the present and reduces history, cosmology, and eschatology to anthropology.

Bultmann proceeds to reinterpret Paul's eschatology so that it is separated from apocalypticism. The apocalyptic elements that remain are considered by Bultmann to be products of the first century worldview. As such they are no longer meaningful to the scientifically oriented modern human and are part of the mythology of the New Testament.[42] To make these elements clear and understandable they must

---

[39] Bultmann, *Theology of the New Testament*, I, pp. 199-204, 252-53.

[40] Bultmann, 'History and Eschatology in the New Testament', *New Testament Studies* 1 (1954-55), p. 13. This is in contrast to Schweitzer who maintained that as a result of the delayed *parousia* history has swallowed up eschatology.

[41] Bultmann, *The Presence of Eternity*, p. 43.

[42] Bultmann, 'The New Testament and Mythology', pp. 15-16, contends that the essence of New Testament mythology is Jewish apocalyptic and the Gnostic redemption myths and that common to both are such features as dualism, divine intervention as integral to the redemption, and cosmic catastrophes.

The definition of mythology is one about which there has been a great deal of debate. Mythology, as used by Bultmann, refers to those forms in which the divine is spoken of in terms of the human, the other worldly in terms of this world and human existence in terms of an objectifying view. See Bultmann, 'The New Testament and Mythology', pp. 10-11, and Rudolf Bultmann, 'On the Problem of Demythologizing', in Richard Batey (ed.), *New Testament Issues* (New York: Harper and Row, 1970), pp. 35-44. In general, there have been three criticisms of Bultmann raised: (1) His definition excludes much language essential to religious expression and without which there could be no real theology. (2) The definition separates the form from the content. (3) Bultmann himself has been inconsistent in the

be interpreted in terms of the themes of human existence, i.e. the mythological thinking must be interpreted existentially and the meaning of this thinking is determined by what it reflects about the understanding of humanity's existence.[43] Once the apocalyptic concepts have been interpreted existentially they are, according to Bultmann, of no further value in understanding the New Testament. For him apocalyptic symbols have only a remnant of significance, which, however, is not found in a literal future but in the mode of response (faith) to the proclamation of Christ. Thus, he writes off apocalypticism as not meeting with the existential interpretation and proposes that it is no further value because the *parousia* never took place.[44]

Since the apocalyptic scheme of the two ages is a central concern in our study of 1 Corinthians, let us pursue Bultmann's application of his program to Paul's doctrine of the two ages. As we have already

---

application of the definition, i.e., he treats some forms as mythology which do not fit the definition. Reservations regarding Bultmann's approach have come from a number of quarters. In his article 'Entmythologisierung als Aufgabe der Christologie', *Evangelische Theologie* 26 (1966), pp. 349-68, Ulrich Luz contends that Bultmann understands myth from the modern standpoint that disregards the original intention of myth. That intention was not to present an objective description of the world but to portray a certain way of understanding and experiencing the world that can only be adequately expressed in that form. Thus, Bultmann takes a contemporary conception of myth and applies that understanding in his effort to replace what he considers to be mythical elements in the New Testament by a more scientific concept. Still another critic of Bultmann is Ernst Lohmeyer, who in 'The Right Interpretation of the Mythological', *Kerygma and Myth*, p. 128, finds that the existential interpretation is inadequate to deal with the full range of the relationship between God and the world, which is almost more important. Bultmann in his interpretation limits the importance of the world to providing a stage for human existence. As well as humanity, God is the center of the world. Human life, furthermore, is just one element in the universe. Though critical of existential interpretation neither Luz nor Lohmeyer offers a more adequate means of interpretation. Julius Schniewind in 'A Reply to Bultmann', *Kerygma and Myth*, p. 49, asks, 'Is the human mind really capable of dispensing with myth?'

[43] The problem centers around Bultmann's attempt to explicate the message or, as he puts it, to expose the real *scandalon* of the New Testament so that it becomes clear to modern humanity.

[44] Bultmann, 'The New Testament and Mythology', *Kerygma and Myth*, p. 5. In 'History and Eschatology in the New Testament', Bultmann asserts,

The true solution of the problem (non-occurrence of the *parousia*) lies in the thought of Paul and John, namely in the idea that Christ is the ever present or ever becoming present eschatological event. That is to say, that the New gets character by the encounter with Christ or with the Word which proclaims him, because in the encounter with Him the world and its history comes to its end and the believer becomes free from the world by becoming a new creature.

noted, Bultmann does not think that Paul departed completely from Jewish tradition. Bultmann recognizes that the primitive church, Paul included, interpreted its time in terms of the apocalyptic scheme of the two ages, i.e. humanity between the times is waiting for the breaking of the new age at the *parousia* of Christ; but he understands that while Paul retains the terminology of two ages, the Apostle reinterprets the apocalyptic scheme so that its significance lies in the present. The eschatological event has already occurred for the Christian.[45]

Salvation is understood to occur in the Christ-event, which is an eschatological act of God that stands outside of all temporal limitations and historical events.[46] This saving occurence ends the old aeon and introduces the new aeon.[47] By this the person of faith is dehistoricized by release from the previous ties of history and is placed at the brink of the end.[48] Consequently Bultmann maintains that the church is an eschatological community of those who are divorced from the world. As such it is not a phenomenon of the world and its history; it belongs to the new age. Yet the church is an entity within the world and its history. The members of the church live between the resurrection and the *parousia* of Christ. In the 'time-between' they find their existence to be ambiguous.[49] While they live in the present reality of eschatological righteousness and life, sin and death are still present realities. They are in the world and part of its history, but they have their existence apart from the world. The double character of their salvation lies in the fact that it 'already' belongs to the new aeon, but the eschatological existence of Christian community is 'yet' to be

---

[45] Bultmann, *Presence of Eternity*, pp. 42, 43.

[46] Bultmann, *Theology of the New Testament*, I, p. 303. The eschatological event is an event in history, beginning with the appearance of Jesus Christ; but even though it happened as a historical event in the past, at the same time it is an eternal event. It remains in continuity with the historical event and occurs again and again in the Christian's faith. Every instant has the possibility of being an eschatological instant and in the Christian faith this possibility is realized. Bultmann, *The Presence of Eternity*, p. 154. As an eschatological event it never becomes merely a fact of the past and cannot be confirmed by historical processes which can be determined with certainty. No historical document can disclose the salvation occurrence. It stands outside of time and constantly takes place in the present moment in both the proclamation of the gospel and in the sacraments (Bultmann, *The Presence of Eternity*, p. 138).

[47] Bultmann, *Theology of the New Testament*, I, p. 278.

[48] Bultmann, *Theology of the New Testament*, I, p. 25.

[49] Bultmann, *Theology of the New Testament*, I, p. 308.

realized.[50] At the personal level of Christian existence the dialectic of 'already-not yet' is expressed in the relation of the indicative and the imperative. 'The believer must still become what he already is, and he is already what he shall become.'[51]

What is significant for the existence of the believer, according to Bultmann, is not the world with its temporal past or future but the eschatological 'now' where the person of faith hears the demand of God and is granted the possibility of authentic self-understanding and existence. Whereas Jewish thought anticipated God's righteousness (δικαιοσύνη) to be a future verdict in the eschatological judgment, Paul, so Bultmann notes, uses δικαιοσύνη also as a forensic-eschatological term; but he breaks with Jewish tradition in his emphasis on righteousness as present realization.[52] Because of the salvation occurrence Christ's righteousness through faith becomes a present reality for the hearer of the gospel: 'God already pronounces His eschatological verdict (over the man of faith) in the present; the eschatological event is already present reality, or rather is beginning in the present.'[53]

The contrast between Paul and Jewish traditional conception of righteousness does not lie in any fundamental disagreement regarding its forensic eschatological nature but in the time of its revelation. While in Jewish thought it is expected in the future, in Pauline thought the eschatological event has occurred, and righteousness is already imputed to the person of faith.[54]

---

[50] Bultmann, *Theology of the New Testament*, I, pp. 278-79.

[51] Bultmann, *The Presence of Eternity*, p. 48. See Rudolf Bultmann, *The Old and the New Man in the Letters of Paul* (trans. Keith R. Crim; Richmond: John Knox Press, 1967), pp. 16-17.

[52] Bultmann, *Theology of the New Testament*, I, pp. 272-73. While Bultmann recognizes that δικαιοσύνη in Rom. 2.13 and Gal. 5.5 is used in the traditional sense of a future verdict in the coming judgment, he considers that such passages as Rom. 1.17; 5.1, 21; 8.10, 30; 1 Cor. 6.11 demonstrate that Paul stresses the present reality of eschatological righteousness, and furthermore, that the future tenses of Rom. 3.20 and 3.30 probably are not genuine futures but gnomic futures and that the present tenses of Gal. 2.16; 3.11; 5.4 are not genuine presents but timeless presents (Bultmann, *Theology of the New Testament*, I, pp. 274-75.).

[53] Bultmann, *Theology of the New Testament*, I, p. 276.

[54] Bultmann makes it clear that righteousness should not be understood as a quality of the believer's existence but in terms of the dialectical tension between the 'already' and the 'not yet'. 'The "righteousness" which is the goal of "faith" is no quality which adheres to humanity but is humanity's relation to God. If it has become a present possibility, this "present-ness" is not a temporal and therefore a

Obviously Bultmann understands that Paul has radically individu-
alized the apocalyptic doctrine of the two-ages. For him this means
not only does Paul abandon the cosmic view of redemption but also
the strong futuristic emphasis in Jewish apocalyptic so that in the
Apostle's thought the emphasis falls on the present participation of
the Christian in the new age. While Bultmann recognizes that Paul
retains the apocalyptic motif of the ages, he sees Paul so reinterpret-
ing it that a chronological scheme is unimportant. The death and resurrection of Christ is the salvific event; the old aeon has come to an
end for the Christian and the new aeon of redemption has been established. Though remnants of apocalypticism are found in Paul's
thought, Bultmann suggests that these are peripheral to the understanding of the Apostle's message. The Apostle has decisively modified the apocalyptic perspective and current eschatology to apply only
to the present experience of humanity: 'Paul has interpreted the apocalyptic view of history on the basis of anthropology. The Pauline view
of history is the expression of his view of man.'[55]

> He (Paul) cannot regard the eschatological consummation as the
> completion of the history of the Jewish nation, not even in the
> extended form depicted in Deutero-Isaiah and some later Jewish
> visions of the eschatological hope, namely, that the welfare of Is-
> rael is at the same time the welfare of all peoples. On the contrary,
> his conception of the eschatological bliss is also determined by
> his anthropology.[56]

Bultmann's interpretation of the two-age scheme in Pauline
thought eliminates the cosmological and corporate concerns of redemption and eschatology. In Paul the two-ages, having nothing to
do fundamentally with the themes of a dramatic cosmic catastrophe
and renewal of the cosmos at a denouement,[57] apply only to the existential situation of the individual Christian. 'Eschatology has wholly

---

temporary state. Rather, its 'present-ness' is that of the eschatological Now. That
is, it is always both here and ahead of the already right-wised believer as future to
him' (Bultmann, *Theology of the New Testament*, I, p. 319). Thus, eschatological existence is not a new nature that is conferred upon the believer; it must be renewed
habitually in new decision and obedience.

[55] Bultmann, *The Presence of Eternity*, p. 41.

[56] Bultmann, *The Presence of Eternity*, p. 42.

[57] Bultmann observes, however, that Paul retains the expectations of future
cosmic events, but that John has given them up. See *The Presence of Eternity*, p. 47.

lost its sense of goal of history and is, in fact, understood as the goal of the individual human being.'[58] In other words, humanity's redemption does not wait for some final event; the Apostle has transcended the temporal dualistic distinctions common in Jewish apocalyptic and understands that the Christian's redemption does not lie in some event in the future but that the end of the old age and the introduction of the new age occurred with the events of Jesus and continue to occur for humans by their acceptance of the word of preaching.[59]

> In his faith he (the Christian) is already above time and history. For although the advent of Christ is an historical event which happened 'once' in the past, it is at the same, an eternal event which occurred again and again in the soul of any Christian … In his faith he is a contemporary of Christ and time and the world's history are overcome.[60]

To summarize, Bultmann interprets Paul's eschatology so that God is fulfilling his 'historical' purpose in the experience of the individual. The old aeon for the Christian has come to an end. The Christian's past as a sinner has been terminated. The new aeon is not a future hope of Christians, for they experience within themselves the life of the new age.[61] Therefore, the new age is not understood by Paul, according to Bultmann, to be determined by any future event such as the *parousia* nor does the temporal future play any significant role in Pauline eschatology.

C.H. Dodd

Dodd has made fundamental to his interpretation of Pauline eschatology his understanding of the primitive Christian *kerygma*. He recognizes that the temporal expectation of an apocalyptic end had deep roots in the belief of the primitive Christians. In the earliest days they proclaimed the 'immediate' advent of Christ, but as a consequence of the non-occurrence of the *parousia* it was necessary for them to alter

---

[58] Bultmann, 'History and Eschatology in the New Testament', p. 13.

[59] Bultmann, *Theology of the New Testament*, I, p. 302.

[60] Bultmann, *The Presence of Eternity*, p. 153. Bultmann cites here Eric Frank, 'The Role of History in Christian Thought', in L. Edelstein (ed.), *Knowledge, Will and Belief: Collected Essays* (Zurich: Artemis-Verlag, 1955), pp. 74, 75.

[61] Bultmann seems to allow, at least theoretically, for two ages to exist concurrently. Cf. *Theology of the New Testament* I, pp. 299-300, pp. 349.

the perspective of the *kerygma*, particularly the imminent expectation of the advent of the Lord.[62] In his reconstruction of the *kerygma* Dodd concludes that for Paul and the Jerusalem church 'the decisive thing had already happened',[63] and thus in the first century the apocalyptic expectation began to vanish with the main burden of apostolic preaching resting on the new age as already a present reality.[64]

This line of eschatological development is seen by Dodd in Paul's letters where he detects that Paul outgrew apocalyptic and came to center his *kerygma* on the death and resurrection of Christ 'as the divinely ordained crisis in history through which old things passed away and the new order came into being'.[65] Dodd finds support for his argument that Paul's theological position corresponds with the primitive *kerygma* by detecting in Paul's career evidence of theological development, particularly marked by a shift away from an apocalyptic *Weltanschauung*.

Furthermore, he sees a correlation between Paul's revision of eschatology and a spiritual change, 'a sort of second conversion'[66] between the writing of 2 Cor. 10-13 and 2 Cor. 1-9. This spiritual crisis arose out of the trouble that Paul had with the Corinthian church and led him to surrender his apocalyptic world-view. The change wrought in Paul's character and attitude toward the world by this experience

---

[62] C.H. Dodd, *The Apostolic Preaching and Its Developments* (New York: Harper and Row, 1964), pp. 31-33. Dodd argues, 'In the earliest days it was possible to hold to the conviction in the indivisible unity of an experience which included also the expectation of an immediate overt confirmation of its truth … As time went on, the indivisible unity of experience which lay behind the preaching of the apostles was broken. The Lord did not come on the clouds', (Dodd, *The Apostolic Preaching and Its Developments,* p. 34).

[63] Dodd, *The Apostolic Preaching and Its Developments,* p. 32. *In The Parables of the Kingdom* (London: Nisbet and Company, 1935), p. 108, C.H. Dodd maintains that apocalyptists used language symbolically and that the future tenses in the teaching of Jesus were nothing more than an accommodation of language. The kingdom is not something that will happen after other things occur. There is, according to Dodd, no before or after in the eternal order.

[64] Dodd, *The Apostolic Preaching and Its Developments,* p. 85, draws from his examination of a number of passages in the New Testament this conclusion: 'For the New Testament writers in general, the eschaton has entered history; the hidden rule of God has been revealed; the age to come has come. The Gospel of primitive Christianity is a Gospel of realized eschatology.'

[65] Dodd, *The Apostolic Preaching and Its Developments,* p. 43.

[66] C.H. Dodd, 'The Mind of Paul: I' (New Testament Studies; Manchester: The University Press, 1953), p. 81.

is reflected in his epistles written subsequent to 2 Cor. 10-13 including part of a letter preserved in 2 Cor. 1-9.[67] Dodd explains this:

> It is at any rate plain that in later epistles there is a change of temper. The traces of fanaticism and intolerance disappeared, almost if not quite completely, along with all that anxious insistence on his own dignity. The new temper shows itself in the way in which the controversies of Romans and Colossians are conducted, in a generous recognition of the natural virtues of mankind, in a sense of the values of ordinary family (which he had once depreciated as belonging to 'the things of the world') and in a sustained emphasis on the idea of reconciliation. It is in the epistle of the Philippians (possibly the last of his letters which we possess in an interpolated form) that we see most clearly what experience had made of this naturally proud, self-assertive, and impatient man. 'I do not reckon myself', he says, to have attained. I am pressing on towards the mark.[68]

From this exposition it becomes clear that for Dodd the spiritual crisis represents not only a conversion away from the impatience of an apocalyptic temperament but also a shift in Paul's theological stance, i.e. a fundamental revision of eschatology, 'involving the revaluation of the natural order'.[69]

In tracing the stages that led Paul to abandon the *Weltanschauung* of apocalyptic and to revise his eschatology Dodd proposes the following: When Paul was converted, he brought with him the apocalyptic distinction between 'this age' and 'the age to come'. As a Christian the initial stage of his eschatological stance was best represented by the Book of Enoch, the Apocalypse of Baruch, and the Apocalypse of Ezra – Jewish writings that draw attention to the expectation that the present world order ('this age'), which is under demonic powers, will be radically renewed and the enemies of God destroyed when the new order ('the age to come') comes about by a catastrophic divine intervention. Though Paul believed that the age to come had

---

[67] Dodd, 'The Mind of Paul', p. 80.
[68] Dodd, 'The Mind of Paul', p. 81.
[69] Dodd, 'The Mind of Paul: II', p. 126. Dodd detects changes in two aspects of Paul's thought: '(1) eschatology and the valuation of the natural order, and (2) the universality of the Christian religion' (Dodd, 'The Mind of Paul: II', pp. 108-109). Our principal concern here is Dodd's detection of changes in Pauline eschatology.

been inaugurated by the resurrection of Christ, he maintained the belief that the *parousia* of Christ would bring fully the new age. At first then he adapted his new beliefs to the apocalyptic framework of the doctrine of the two ages.[70]

According to Dodd the initial state of Paul's eschatology is reflected in his earlier letters, namely, the Thessalonian correspondence, 1 Corinthians and 1 Corinthians 10-13.[71] These letters teach absolute dualism – 'the dualism of "things of the Lord" and "things of the world", of "this age" and "the age to come", of the "elect" and the rest of humanity, of redeemed humanity and the whole living universe'.[72] However, Dodd suggests that though the earlier letters retain the essential features of apocalyptic, there is evidence of an unmistakable change in emphasis in 1 Corinthians. There is nothing said of

---

[70] Dodd, 'The Mind of Paul: II', p. 109.

[71] Dodd is not the only one to argue that Pauline eschatology shows signs of the development and to group Paul's letters in terms of the stages of the development. R.H. Charles, *Eschatology: the Doctrine of the Future Life in Israel, Judaism and Christianity* (New York: Schocken Books, 1963), p. 437, states, 'He (Paul) began with an expectation of the future that he had inherited largely from Judaism, but under the influence of great formative Christian conceptions he parted gradually from this and on a process of development'. Charles works out four stages in this development and groups the letters accordingly: (1) the Thessalonian correspondence; (2) 1 Corinthians; (3) 2 Corinthians and Romans; (4) Philippians, Colossians and Ephesians (Charles, *Eschatology*, pp. 437-73). The first edition of the work by Charles mentioned above was published in 1899. As Dodd, Charles contends that the Apostle began with traditional eschatological expectations of Judaism. However, he suggests that in the first two phases of his growth Paul continued to believe in the necessity of the *parousia* for humanity's salvation but that while Paul never completely abandoned the *parousia* hope, for the most part he relinquished the Jewish expectation that placed so much stress on the *parousia* and the future kingdom of God (Charles, *Eschatology*, p. 56). Dodd's and Charles' hypothesis that Paul matured in his conception of Christianity and outgrew apocalyptic fails to convince for two reasons: (1) the evidence cited from letters does not clearly attest that there were fundamental shifts in Paul's thought; (2) neither Dodd nor Charles take seriously the occasions for Paul's letters. Crucial to the interpretation of Paul's letters is cognizance that Paul was engaged in polemics and that Paul's controlling purpose is not to expound his views except as they were pertinent to an opposing position. However, Charles Buck and Greer Taylor, *Saint Paul* (New York: Charles Scribner's Sons, 1969), have argued quite persuasively for a fundamental shift in Paul's eschatological outlook.

[72] Dodd, 'The Mind of Paul: II', p. 126. The dualism of 2 Cor. 6.14-7.1 ('The time is short … the fashion of this world is passing away'. vv. 29-31) is typically apocalyptic. But Dodd thinks that this is an interpolation from a letter prior to 1 Corinthians (Dodd, 'The Mind of Paul: II', p. 115).

the Lord's destroying the human enemies of the church as in the Thessalonian letters but only the quasi-personal power, death.[73]

Dodd maintains that Paul in his earlier letters retains the apocalyptic expectation of the nearness of the *parousia*, but he detects in this initial stage 'a slight change of emphasis,' namely that in 1 Thessalonians the death of the believer before the *parousia* is the exception, but in 1 Corinthians Paul assures 'his readers not all Christians will die'.[74] After 1 Corinthians Paul abandons the expectation that the *parousia* was imminent. As a result of this development, 'we hear no more of that confident expectation, so far at least as Paul himself is concerned'.[75] That is, Dodd maintains that the motif of the *parousia* does appear in Paul's later letters but that after 1 Corinthians no longer is it expected in his lifetime. While the *parousia* never vanished entirely from Paul's thought, Dodd sees a significant shift in his subsequent letters that devaluates and retires the imminence of the advent into the background.[76]

Paul's movement away from the outlook of an apocalyptic worldview and away from the expectation of the near *parousia* of Christ led him to stress the present status of the believer. As Dodd notes, for Paul the death and the resurrection marked the transition from 'this age' to the age to come'.[77] Thus understanding that the new age began with Jesus, Paul abandoned the nearness motif and emphasized that the kingdom was already present and that the believer lived in the new age here and now. Dodd sees the delay of the *parousia* as fundamental to this change in outlook. He goes on to explain:

> … If the Advent is deferred to an indefinite future, then the present gains in significance. And as we have seen, side by side with the diminishing emphasis on the imminence of the Advent goes a growing emphasis on the eternal life here and now in communion with Christ.[78]

---

[73] Dodd, 'The Mind of Paul: II', p. 122.
[74] Dodd, 'The Mind of Paul: II', p. 110.
[75] Dodd, 'The Mind of Paul: II', p. 110.
[76] Though Dodd does not find any remnant of an impatient apocalyptic expectation in Colossians, Ephesians and Philippians, he takes note of Rom. 13.11-14 with 1 Thess. 5.1-11 but concludes that the two passages are quite different in tone and that throughout Romans there is no appeal to an imminent *parousia* (Dodd, 'The Mind of Paul: II', p. 111).
[77] Dodd, *The Apostolic Preaching and Its Developments*, p. 13.
[78] Dodd, 'The Mind of Paul: II', pp. 112-13.

If we assume this interpretation is correct the Christian already lives the heavenly life which for Dodd is the same as living in the new age[79] and Paul has shifted the present and future eschatology with which he began toward a present eschatology so that the focal interest becomes 'all the riches of divine grace enjoyed here and now by those who are in Jesus Christ'.[80] This represents a decisive transformation of eschatology into mysticism. That is, as the Apostle's interest in the speedy return of Christ declines, 'the "futuristist eschatology" of his earlier phase is replaced by … Christ-mysticism'.[81] Consequently the term 'Christ-mysticism' is used by Dodd to describe the present life of the Christian in the new age and stands in contrast to the futuristic expectations shared by Jewish apocalyptic and Paul's predecessors in the church. To use Dodd's words:

> It is in the epistles of Paul, therefore, that full justice is done for the first time to the principle of 'realized eschatology' which is vital to the whole *kerygma*. That supernatural order of life which the apocalyptists had predicted in terms of pure fantasy is now described as an actual fact of experience.[82]

In terms of Dodd's understanding Paul has radically reinterpreted the two-age motif by stressing the *here* and *now* and supplanting '… if the apocalyptic eschatology which moulded the *Weltanschauung* with which Paul began'[83] with 'realized eschatology'. Christ-mysticism represents, therefore, a reinterpretation of eschatology so that the temporal dualistic limitations of Jewish apocalyptic are transcended[84] and the two-ages now refer to present experience of whether or not one is 'in Christ'. The new age is already here by virtue of Christ's death and resurrection. A new order, which makes it clear that history subsequent to the coming of Christ is qualitatively different from history prior to the incarnation is the order in which Christians live now

---

[79] Dodd, 'The Mind of Paul: II', p. 112.
[80] Dodd, *The Apostolic Preaching and Its Developments*, p. 13.
[81] Dodd, *The Apostolic Preaching and Its Developments*, p. 13. Cf. Dodd, 'The Mind of Paul: II', p. 113.
[82] Dodd, *The Apostolic Preaching and Its Developments*, p. 65.
[83] Dodd, 'The Mind of Paul: II', p. 126.
[84] Cf. Dodd, *The Apostolic Preaching and It's Developments*, p. 68, and 'The Mind of Paul: II', p. 126.

while in this earthly existence. Dodd cites Col. 3.3, 'You are dead and your life is hid with Christ in God'.[85]

In maintaining that the divine purpose is being worked out within the field of recorded history, Dodd notes that the Old Testament prophets believed that the Day of the Lord would be the last in the historical series, yet the radical contrast between 'this age' and 'the age to come' is made clear by the prophetic description of the 'Day of the Lord' in terms which remove it from the conditions of time and space.[86] The New Testament employs the symbolism of the Old, but from an entirely different perspective. Through the ministry, death and resurrection of Jesus the divine event was understood to have happened and 'the meaning of history is now summed up'.[87] Because the divine event is realized in the realm of history, Dodd finds it necessary to speak of two kinds of history, empirical history and sacred history. While they exist at the same time, they are not necessarily the same. Empirical history is the events of the ages. It is the events of the temporal and historical order and the plane where men live the earthly life. Sacred history is distinguished by its absolute and final quality. The New Testament insists on the uniqueness and finality of the ministry, death, and resurrection of Christ. These took place under Pontius Pilate in the first century, but the early church understood them to be more than historical facts. They are regarded as events in which God manifestly entered history. The New Testament writers maintain that in the death of Jesus there was an unparalleled encounter between God and the forces of evil. From the events of Christ's death and resurrection emerged a new kind of life for mankind, and history has been qualitatively different from what it was before the coming of Christ. This sacred history signifies not an absolute temporal end to history, but the essence of its meaning for the Christian lies in what Dodd describes as 'realized eschatology'. 'The age to come' has come; sacred history has been consummated. The events of Jesus are not

> … anything short of the unique and absolute entrance of the Kingdom of God, the eschaton, into human experience. 'The

---

[85] Dodd, *The Apostolic Preaching and Its Development*, p. 88.
[86] Dodd, *The Apostolic Preaching and Its Development*, pp. 80-81
[87] Dodd, *The Apostolic Preaching and Its Development*, p. 85. Dodd goes on to say, 'There remains a residue of eschatology which is not exhausted in the "realized eschatology" of the Gospel, namely, the element of sheer finality' (p. 93).

Word was made flesh': no more absolute revelation of God to history than that can be conceived.[88]

Ernst Käsemann

Criticism of Bultmann's separation of Paul's apocalypticism from his eschatology has been heard within the Bultmannian school. In particular Ernst Käsemann, insisting that apocalypticism with its cosmological and corporate dimensions is the constitutive factor in Paul's thought, complains that Bultmann has reduced Paul's theology too exclusively to an 'anthropology'.[89] Käsemann along with Schweitzer, has called attention to the prime importance of apocalyptic in Pauline eschatology and to redemption that is radically conceived by Paul to include the cosmos as well as humanity. His purpose has been to demonstrate that Christian theology, including Paul's thought, has its origins in apocalypticism.[90]

---

[88] Dodd, *The Apostolic Preaching and Its Development*, p. 93.

[89] See Käsemann's, 'The Beginnings of Christian Theology', pp. 44-45, 'On the Topic of Primitive Christian Apocalyptic', in Robert W. Funk (ed.), *Apocalypticism* (Journal for Theology and the Church 6; New York: Herder and Herder, 1969), pp. 118-19, and 'The Righteousness of God in Paul', *New Testament Questions of Today*, pp. 168-82. Käsemann's understanding of apocalypticism has led him to oppose a consistent existential interpretation and to insist on the recovery of apocalypticism. He feels that existential interpretation fails to exhaust the meaning of apocalyptic and is unwilling to dismiss apocalypticism as readily as Bultmann does.

[90] See *supra*, note 2. Käsemann has been challenged by Rudolf Bultmann in 'Ist Apocalyptic die Mutter des christlichen Theologie?', in *Apophoreta: Festschrift für Ernst Haenchen* (Berlin: Alfred Topelmann Verlag, 1964). Bultmann maintains that eschatology rather than apocalypticism is the 'mother' of Christian theology. Käsemann feels that the Gospel of Matthew offers support for his premise that apocalyptic is the controlling factor in the thought structure of primitive Christianity. He postulates that there was already in earliest confessional Christianity at least two opposing eschatologies: (1) There was one group who tried to maintain ties with late Jewish hopes. This group saw their primary purpose of proclamation to try to get Israel back together first, before a gentile mission was started. In fact, for them, the gentile mission could not come into being until Israel was back on right terms with God through Christ. Because of their ties with late Judaism and the prophetic nature of this proclamation, this group tended to use quite extensively eschatological language with its emphasis upon divine law curse and blessing, exhortation, comfort, promise, etc. Matthew, being disposed to this rabbinic tradition, later picks up this group's *logia* and preserves their apocalyptic-eschatological proclamation. (2) Over against the above group was another group of early Christians who confessionally held another eschatology. This group by and large, according to Käsemann, disregards the tradition of their Jewish fathers and moves out in a new

In the fourth essay in *Apocalypticism* Käsemann responds to the criticism of Ebeling and Fuchs of his 'The Beginnings of Christian Theology' with an outline of the development of post-Easter apocalyptic up to Paul. He maintains that Paul remained aligned with the apocalyptic *Weltanschauung* throughout his life and ministry and that the Apostle appealed to apocalyptic theology as a corrective to the incursions of eschatological enthusiasm into the church. A model illustration of this, according to Käsemann, is the church in Corinth where the cause of all the disorders was the view of the dominant group that complete redemption had already taken place. The theology of the enthusiasts is summed up by Käsemann: 'As participators in the cross of Christ, the baptized are at the same time also participators in the resurrection and enthronement of Christ; they have been liberated from the old eon of the kingdom of Christ.'[91] The radical understanding that the redeemed are risen and enthroned with Christ in heaven was ground for the belief that the end of history had already come. Imagining that all that apocalyptic hoped for – including the resurrection body supposedly conferred by baptism and entrance of the redeemed into an angel-like state – were realized, the enthusiasts believed that their new-found heavenly life should not be restricted by the earthly order.[92] They understood that Christ as the new cosmocrator in his resurrection and enthronement had dethroned the cosmic powers reigning in the world and that He had entered upon his sovereignty that extended throughout the world. For them the *eschaton* had arrived; the Holy Spirit and the *charismata* proved the reality of the eschatological event and the occurrence of the new creation.[93]

---

mission, a gentile mission after Easter and the receiving of the Spirit. This group possibly was Stephen's group of seven.

The Jewish-Christian group centered around Jerusalem where they became legalistic. The liberal group centered around Antioch where Paul later developed his ministry. But Käsemann feels that there was a group of Jewish-Christians who did not become tied to legalistic Jerusalem but lived in and around Syria-Palestine. Here they maintained the Jewish-Christian apocalyptical proclamation through various forms of eschatological prophetic statements which keeps them in line again with late Judaism and its hopes. Especially, Käsemann feels, does this group view the end-times, the enthronement of God and of Christ as the eschatological Son of Man and/or the proof of the righteousness of God as grounded in apocalyptic. Käsemann, 'The Beginnings of Christian Theology', pp. 17-46.

[91] Käsemann, 'On the Topic of Primitive Christian Apocalyptic', p. 119.

[92] Käsemann, 'On the Topic of Primitive Christian Apocalyptic', pp. 120, 125.

[93] Käsemann, 'On the Topic of Primitive Christian Apocalyptic', pp. 122-24.

This theological outlook, especially the attempt to demonstrate the reality of new found heavenly freedom in the world, Käsemann claims, 'lies at the root of the disorders in Corinth – the contempt for discipline and morals, the lack of consideration for the weaker brethren at the Lord's Supper and in the life of everyday, the revolt of the women who had ecstatic gifts, the over-rating of speaking with tongues and of sexual asceticism, which are regarded as evidences of angel-like being'.[94]

Furthermore, Käsemann feels that he can find, particularly in 1 Cor. 15.20-28, support for the premise that Paul, by the use of apocalyptic, limits the over-realized eschatology of the enthusiasts. As a safeguard against the present eschatology of the enthusiasts Paul, Käsemann explains, introduces an eschatological reservation: the consummation is still outstanding. The Apostle shapes eschatology in terms of the dialectic of 'already-not yet' and thus makes it necessary that his eschatological thought be seen in its double aspect.

Paul's present eschatology is described by Käsemann as *basileia Christi*, a term borrowed from apocalyptic. Since Easter, the eschatological subjection of the cosmic powers has been in process and the end of it is imminent. Salvation appears as already present by faith and baptism, but the general resurrection lies in the future. Contrary to his enthusiastic opponents Paul maintains that the *basileia Christi* is provisional and limited and therefore, decisively asserts the apocalyptic reservation: 'not yet' is the world wholly subject to God, and the end of history has not come.[95]

From the above the conclusion might be drawn that apocalyptic tradition was merely a tool used by Paul to serve his polemical interests, but on the contrary Käsemann contends that it is central to Pauline thought. 'Even when he became a Christian, Paul remained an apocalyptist.'[96] Paul's apostolic self-consciousness and his method

---

[94] Käsemann, 'On the Topic of Primitive Christian Apocalyptic', p. 120.

[95] Käsemann, 'On the Topic of Primitive Christian Apocalyptic', pp. 128-29. Cf. also '"The Righteousness of God" in Paul', pp. 170-71.

[96] Käsemann, 'On the Topic of Primitive Christian Apocalyptic', p. 181. Käsemann recognizes that what distinguishes Paul's theology from Jewish tradition is the Christological orientation. Consequently, there is no attempt to divorce Paul from the Christian context. The Apostle does not stand in a Jewish context; he already lives in the messianic era. Betz, 'The Concept of Apocalyptic in the Pannenberg Group', p. 205, calls attention to the 'need to distinguish between the Christian apocalyptic ideas of Paul and Jewish apocalypticism'. I can concur with Betz provided he does not mean that apocalyptic tradition was just a carry-over

and goal are comprehensible only in terms of his apocalyptic.[97] More-over, he argues that Paul's present eschatology should not necessarily be seen as an innovation or break with Jewish tradition. Detecting in the Thanksgiving Psalms from Qumran a stress on 'realized escahtol-ogy' Käsemann says, 'he (Paul) still stands basically within the possi-bilities and realities at least of one particular stream of Jewish apoca-lyptic'.[98]

Paul's cosmology is fundamental to his eschatology and his char-acteristic view is that the divine will for salvation is directed not pri-marily towards the individual but towards the whole world. Signifi-cant in this regard, so Käsemann thinks, are the references in Paul to the cosmic powers reigning in the world. Christ, exalted to the right hand of God, is sovereign over all world powers, with the exception of death, upon the earth. In the church – but only in the church – the powers, except death, have suffered the loss of the lordship of Christ.[99] Christian existence involves a change of lordship. Thus, hu-manity is never free in the sense of being autonomous; rather, hu-manity must choose between the lordship of the powers and the lord-ship of Christ.[100] Visible expression of Christ's lordship is in the

---

from the Apostle's past and that he never did incorporate it into his Christian think-ing so that it was fundamental to his theology. Furthermore, Bruce Vawter insists that though 'Christian apocalyptic differs from the Jewish, it has not ceased to be apocalyptic'. 'And He Shall Come Again with Glory: Paul and Christian Apocalyp-tic', in *Studiorum Paulinorum Congressus Internationalis Catholicus 1961* (Analecta Biblica 17-18; Rome: E. Pontificco Instituto Biblico, 1963), p. 127.

[97] Käsemann, 'On the Topic of Primitive Christian Apocalyptic', p. 126.

[98] Käsemann, '"The Righteousness of God" in Paul', p. 178. Cf. Calvin J. Roet-zel, *Judgment in the Community* (Leiden: Brill, 1972), pp. 72-85. He agrees with Käse-mann that the background of Paul's doctrine of righteousness is apocalypticism but takes issue with Käsemann's contention that the Thanksgiving Psalms of Qum-ran offer evidence that already in apocalyptic Judaism the present manifestation of God's righteousness is comparable to the Pauline emphasis. While the psalmist can speak of God who is now righteous, Roetzel rightly observes that in contrast to Paul the Qumran texts view the final vindication of God's righteousness as still outstanding and still remaining in the imminent future. Moreover, while a degree of overlap of the ages may be detected in the Qumran outlook, for Paul the time is later. The Messiah had come. The eschatological day is already present in some sense.

[99] Käsemann, 'On the Topic of Primitive Christian Apocalyptic', pp. 128-29. The powers still reign in the world that surrounds the church but in view of the teaching of the Christological hymn of col. 1.15-20 there seems to be ground for thinking that in some sense Christ's lordship now encompasses the world: δι' αὐτοῦ (Christ) ἀποκαταλλάξαι τὰ πάντα εἰς αὐτόν.

[100] Käsemann, '"The Righteousness of God" in Paul', p. 176.

bodily obedience of the Christian carried out in the daily service of God. The Christian life cannot be restricted to mere inwardness and involves a change of lordship that is more than a mere subjective shift of allegiance from self to Christ.[101]

According to Käsemann then not only is the cosmic perspective basic to Pauline eschatology but more specifically apocalyptic cosmology cannot be separated from Pauline anthropology. For example, he insists that Paul does not primarily employ the technical terms 'spirit' and 'flesh' in a narrow individualistic sense but to characterize the two cosmic spheres which contend for the life of humanity. This is explained by him:

> Man is for Paul never merely himself. Just as he is always a concrete piece of the world, so also what he ultimately is, is determined from without, namely, by the power which takes hold of him and the Lordship to which he surrenders himself. His life is from the start, an object of struggle between God and powers of this world. In other words, it reflects the cosmic struggle for world lordship and is the cyrstallization of it. As such it can be understood only apocalyptically. Thus, what is called the dialectic between the Pauline indicative and imperative, between our already being redeemed and our not yet being secure, is also nothing else but the projection into Christian anthropology of the relation between the Lordship of Christ and the subjection of all cosmic powers.[102]

The apocalyptic concern – God's triumph amid the opposition of the world – is, according to Käsemann, the fundamental issue in the Pauline doctrine of divine righteousness. If this is correct, Paul's conception of the righteousness of God has a broader theological perspective than anthropology. Käsemann expresses it thus: 'δικαιοσύνη θεοῦ is for Paul God's sovereignty over the world, revealing itself eschatologically in Jesus'.[103] That is, God's righteousness is his saving activity[104] and in particular his power that makes his cause to triumph in the world, which has fallen away from him but which, as creation

[101] Käsemann, 'On the Topic of Primitive Christian Apocalyptic', pp. 130-31. Cf. 'The Righteousness of God in Paul', p. 177.
[102] Käsemann, 'On the Topic of Primitive Christian Apocalyptic', p. 132.
[103] Käsemann, '"The Righteousness of God" in Paul', p. 180.
[104] Käsemann, '"The Righteousness of God" in Paul', p. 172.

still belongs to him.[105] Therefore, the righteousness of God, Käsemann believes, 'does not refer primarily to the individual'.[106] In other words anthropology is only part but not the whole of Pauline theology and the justification of the individual human being must be seen in the context of the divine will for the salvation of the entire cosmos. 'God's power', says Käsemann, 'reaches out for the world and the world's salvation lies in its being captured for the sovereignty of God'.[107]

It is apparent that for Käsemann the Pauline doctrine of the righteousness of God is derived from apocalyptic and that it is mainly concerned with the rule of God in the whole world, which was seen by Paul to impinge on his present and could no longer be contemplated as a thing of the distant future. Though it is not to be disclosed universally until the *parousia*, it is realized in the church as the redeemed creation and as the world in obedience to God. Käsemann's exposition, therefore, makes fundamental to the Pauline doctrine of God's righteousness the release from the old aeon and entrance into the new rather than individual forgiveness.[108]

Conclusions and Observations

Since the publication of Johannes Weiss' book *Die Predigt vom Reiche Gottes* the debate has been considerable among biblical scholars concerning the subject of apocalyptic in the New Testament. Weiss was the first to demonstrate decisively that the proclamation of Jesus as well as primitive Christianity, including Paul, was couched in terms of Jewish apocalyptic. The thrust of Paul's eschatological message, according to Weiss, was that the new age has arrived and that the Christian already possesses the fullness of salvation. Pauline

[105] Käsemann, '"The Righteousness of God" in Paul', p. 180.
[106] Käsemann, '"The Righteousness of God" in Paul', p. 180.
[107] Käsemann, '"The Righteousness of God" in Paul', p. 182.
[108] Käsemann, 'The Beginnings of Christian Theology', p. 14, and 'On the Topic of Primitive Christian Apocalyptic', p. 130. He maintains that Paul did modify the apocalyptic scheme of the two ages but not to the extent that he broke with its temporal historical framework as Bultmann suggested. The modification of the apocalyptic scheme is seen by Käsemann to lie in the sharp distinction that Paul makes between the church as the redeemed creation and the world as the unredeemed creation ('On the Topic of Primitive Christian Apocalyptic', p. 130). In what he has published, Käsemann has not attempted to explicate the full significance of the Pauline conception of the two ages.

eschatology represents a break with apocalyptic temporal distinctions and cosmic dimensions and greatly reduces the tension between the 'already-not yet' with stress on the *presentness* of salvation in terms of the Christian's break with a sinful past and entrance into the new age.

Following Weiss, Schweitzer attempted to overcome the apocalyptic nature of primitive Christianity with a theory of thoroughgoing eschatology. He interprets New Testament eschatology as a product of a revision of Jesus' teachings in light of the delay of the *parousia*. While the delay of the *parousia* changed the entire scheme of redemption, Paul's eschatology is consistently dominated by the imminent and apocalyptic expectation of the Kingdom. The Apostle's conviction that the end was at hand was based on the belief that with Jesus the messianic age was introduced and that in his time there was an overlapping of the ages.

However, Schweitzer sees the stress in Paul's eschatology as falling on the temporal and cosmological concerns. Paul envisions redemption to include the cosmos as well as the individual and both a Messianic age which is not realized until the *parousia* and a Kingdom of God which is clearly distinct from the messianic age.

In contrast to Schweitzer but similar to Weiss both Bultmann and Dodd think that the emphasis of Pauline eschatology falls on the fullness of salvation initiated by the Christ-event and that salvation must be understood in highly individualistic terms as inward participation in God's salvation events. While their philosophical base is fundamentally different, Bultmann's and Dodd's conclusions are essentially the same. Both maintain that Paul broke decisively with the apocalyptic scheme of the two ages and taught that what was expected in the *parousia* of Christ was already given in the spiritual experience of the Christians. Therefore, according to them the apocalyptic element (cataclysmic end of history and the world) is not fundamental to Paul's eschatology.

According to Bultmann once apocalyptic forms have been interpreted existentially, they are of no further use in understanding the New Testament. Eschatology is lifted out of the context of apocalyptic with its corporate and cosmological concerns and apocalyptic is marked off as not meeting the existential interpretation. In contrast to Bultmann, Dodd maintains that Paul abandoned the apocalyptic on a developmental thesis. That is, the conviction of the nearness of the *parousia* of Christ with which Paul initially began was modified so that his interest, especially in his later epistles,[109] became that of the present experience of the Christian and the future dimension was radically subordinated to the 'now'.

Weiss, Bultmann, and Dodd see the emphasis of Paul's theology as falling on individual salvation and the present inward participation of the Christian in the powers of the new age. As Schweitzer, Käsemann contends that present eschatology is not the dominating center of Paul's thought but that cosmic and futuristic dimensions of apocalypticism are decisive to Paul's theology. Käsemann understands the Pauline dialectic 'already-not yet' in terms of apocalyptic theology and attempts to hold together both the realized and futuristic dimensions in Pauline eschatology.

As do a number of other scholars Käsemann stresses the correlation between Pauline eschatology and Jewish apocalypticism.[110] He cites 1 Corinthians as a classic example that apocalyptic has left its stamp on the New Testament and that Paul fought eschatological enthusiasm with apocalyptic expectation; but he too, has not systematically explicated the fundamental importance of the apocalyptic scheme of the two ages in this letter and the modification of this scheme by the Christ-event.

Our discussion above reflects that the problem of the functional significance of apocalyptic in Pauline eschatology is far from settled.

---

[109] Dodd, 'The Mind of Paul: II', p. 128, contends that since there are remnants of apocalyptic in 1 Corinthians that it was not until after the composition of this letter that Paul's thought reached its full maturity and that Pauline eschatology must finally be judges in light of its maturity.

[110] H.J. Schoeps, *Paul: the Theology of the Apostle in Light of Jewish History* (trans. Harold Knight; Philadelphia: Westminster Press, 1966), argues that Paul's theology is a christianized Jewish theology. Cf. also Paul Volz, *Die Eschatologie der jüdischen Gemeinde im neutestamentlichen Zeitalter* (Tübingen: J.C.B. Mohr, Verlag, 1934); Hermann Gunkel, *Schöpfung und Chaos in Urzeit und Endzeit* (Göttingen: Vandenhoeck und Ruprecht, 1888); H. St. John Thackerary, *The Relation of St. Paul to Contemporary Jewish Thought* (New York: Macmillan Company, 1900) and Davies, *Paul and Rabbinic Judaism*. In these works and in some commentaries Paul's eschatology is singled out as having a close relation to apocalyptic but none of these including such standard commentaries as Johannes Weiss, *Die Brief an die Korinther* (Meyer Kommentar; Göttingen: Vandenhoech und Ruprecht, 1910); Archibald Robertson and Alfred Plummer, *A Critical Exegetical Commentary on the First Epistle of St. Paul to the Corinthians* (International Critical Commentary; ed. S.R. Driver and others; Edinburgh: T. & T. Clark, 1914), and a more recent one by C.K. Barrett, *The First Epistle to the Corinthians* (Harper's New Testament Commentaries; New York: Harper and Row, 1968) reflect an in-depth study of the function of Jewish apocalyptic in 1 Corinthians.

Though Käsemann might have overstated the case in his contention that 'apocalyptic is the real beginning of primitive Christian theology'[111] the apocalyptic-oriented currents confirm that 'the beginnings of Christianity are closely entwined with Jewish apocalyptic'.[112]

---

[111] Käsemann, 'The Beginning of Christian Theology', p. 40.
[112] Ebeling, 'The Ground of Christian Theology', p. 52.

3

LATE JEWISH APOCALYPTIC

Apocalyptic thought accentuates the coming of the *eschaton*, its description and its attendant circumstances. In his book on Jewish eschatology in the post-Maccabbean period Paul Volz emphasizes the following main themes of apocalyptic: a determinism that has its background in the plan of Yahweh as preached by the Old Testament prophets; the unity of the world in its enmity to God, embodied particularly in the Gentile empires, which were regarded as being in subjection to the power of evil; the activity of God in a supernatural, miraculous form, combined with an emphasis on angels and demons; and a radical dualistic and pessimistic world-view which resulted in a strong other-worldliness and the expectation of imminent judgment and the coming of the new age.[1]

These teachings left their imprint on the beliefs of the primitive church. In the following review of the Jewish apocalyptic, attention is drawn to these theological motifs: the understanding of history, the *Urzeit-Endzeit* scheme, angelic and demonic powers, messianic expectation, and the final judgment. This may provide a backdrop for our exegetical examination of Paul's First Letter to the Corinthians.

The Understanding of History

Unity
Fundamental to the apocalyptists' view of history was the conviction that the divine purpose was being worked out in history, stretching

---

[1] Volz, *Die Eschalogie der judischen Gemeinde im neutestamentlichen Zeitalter*, pp. 4-5.

from creation to consummation.[2] Assuming the imminent end of all things, they survey the whole history of the world in the form of visions and prophecies allegedly given to prominent persons at the beginning of history or at the beginning of other significant periods.[3] 'Their perspective was an indefinitely wider view of the world's history than that of prophecy.'[4] As a corollary to the unity of God as preached by the prophets, they formulated the great conception that all human, cosmological, and spiritual history is a unity,[5] the entire course bound together by the predetermined purpose of God. As a result, the apocalyptists viewed the events as *sub specie aeternitatis*, finding evidence of the divine purpose in the confusion and meaninglessness of history.[6]

While the elaborations of their schemes are somewhat bizarre, in general the apocalyptists take the largest view of things and see all events directed to the establishment of the Kingdom of God. They include in their horizon not only the history of Israel but the entire universe. This is brought out by the writer of the Book of Daniel.[7] In Nebuchadnezzar's dream the great image, which is understood by modern scholarship to represent four great empires, is smashed by a stone (2.31-32). This stone is the eschatological Kingdom of God, which is to replace the earthly kingdoms and which is to become a great mountain and fill the earth (2.35).[8] After the earthly kingdoms are ended, 'the saints of the Most High shall receive the kingdom for ever, for ever and ever' (7.1-2). The horizon of this apocalyptic writer is not limited to Palestine. For him all of history is directed to bring about the imminent establishment of the everlasting kingdom.

The apocalyptists look beyond all temporal limitations and envision that the history of the universe as well as the affairs of humanity are caught up in the cosmic and universal purpose of God. 'From where they stood the apocalyptist could see the past, the present and

---

[2] Russell, *The Method and Message of Jewish Apocalyptic*, pp. 205-206, 263-64.

[3] Philip Vielhauer, 'Apocalyptic', in Hennecke (ed.), *New Testament Apocrypha*, II, p. 592.

[4] Charles, *Eschatology*, p. 205.

[5] Charles, *Eschatology*, p. 205.

[6] Russell, *The Method and Message of Jewish Apocalyptic*, p. 220.

[7] The generally accepted date specifies the Maccabbean age and the reign of Antiochus Epiphanes (175-163 BCE).

[8] All quotations of Scripture are from the Revised Standard Version and of non-canonical apocalyptic literature from Charles (ed.), *Apocrypha and Pseudepigrapha of the Old Testament*.

the future in one continuous perspective. They were not so much conscious of its continuity, however, as they were of its wholeness.'[9]

Dualism

The apocalyptists observed history in terms of the eschaton.[10] Their eschatological understanding of history involves a dualism. The history of the world is seen as a power struggle between God and evil. It is a dualism that is difficult to conceptualize simply in terms of the doctrine of two ontological, co-ordinate, independent principles in the universe. Rather the dualism is the consequence of the experience of present disunity and frustration. 'Common to all true apocalyptic is a situation characterized by anomie, a loss of "world" or erosion of structures, psychic and cultural, with the consequent nakedness of Being or immediacy to the dynamics of existence.'[11] It is the irrationality of the situation that gives rise to the separation between heaven and earth, the righteous and unrighteous, the present and future, and God and the world. This is not just an ontological distinction in a metaphysical sense, but it is a kind of spiritual polarity.[12]

A prominent feature of apocalyptic dualism is the division of all existence into this age and the future age (ὁ αἰὼν οὗτος and ὁ αἰὼν μέλλων). This dualistic time scheme is discernible in the Book of Daniel,[13] where world history is divided sharply into two periods. This is seen in the statue that represents the four-world empires of the first period which stand in contrast to the unhewn stone (Daniel 2). Likewise, the four beasts stand in contrast to the one like unto the son of man (Daniel 7). When God sets up his everlasting kingdom, this world-era with its bestial empires is brought to an end and the rule of the saints begins (cf. Dan. 2.44-45; 7.11-12).[14]

---

[9] Russell, *The Method and Message of Jewish Apocalyptic*, p. 222.

[10] Von Rad, *Old Testament Theology*, II, pp. 304-305. In contrast to the Old Testament prophets' predictions that were from the view of their own day and age and from the present situation, apocalyptic writers observed the past and future.

[11] Amos N. Wilder, 'The Rhetoric of Ancient and Modern Apocalyptic', *Interpretation* 25 (1971), p. 440.

[12] Th. P. van Baaren, 'Toward a Definition of Gnosticism', in Ugo Bianchi (ed.), *Le origini dello Gnosticismo* (Supplements to Numen 12; Leiden: Brill, 1969), p. 117. See 2 Enoch 21.5, 7-8; 228-29; Wisd. Of Sol. 2.24-31.

[13] Cf. von Rad, *Old Testament Theology*, II, pp. 301-302.

[14] Dualistic tendencies also are evident in such prophetic writings as Zechariah 12-14; Joel and Isaiah 24-27, which are older than Daniel. See G.H. Box, 'Jewish Apocalyptic in the Apostolic Age', *The Expositor* 24 (1922), p. 442.

The antithesis between present age and future, between heaven and earth, flowers more in later apocalypses (4 Ezra 4.27; 7.12, 31, 50, 112-114; 2 Baruch 44.9). The age to come is generally regarded as discontinuous with the present world. 'The new world does not turn to corruption (2 Baruch 44.12). 'The ways of the future world are broad and safe and yield the fruit of immortality' (Ezra 7.13).[15] As a consequence of evil's pervading the whole human situation and mastering human nature (4 Ezra 3.22), the present world stands in contrast to the transcendent new age and is doomed to a catastrophic end which was thought to be imminent (4 Ezra 4.41; 5.13). Their negation of this present world led the apocalyptists to anticipate a new heaven and a new earth, a new creation.[16] They contrasted sharply the present and future and saw the 'end' as a termination of the history of the present age which they expected to be superseded by a new age.[17]

The dualism that governs the conception of the two-ages has a qualitative and moral as well as a temporal significance. The opposition of the present evil age to the future age of righteousness comes to clear expression in Daniel 7 and 8: the beasts stand in contrast to the 'man' coming from heaven and the little horn seeks to intrude

---

[15] G.H. Box, 'General Introduction, IV Ezra', in Charles (ed.), *The Apocrypha and Pseudepigrapha of the Old Testament*, pp. 542-43, in dating 4 Ezra says that the *terminus ad quo* for the work of the redactor is 100 CE, and the *terminus ad quem* is 135 CE, the date of the Bar Kokba revolt. It is my opinion that as a historical novel, it draws on the past, so 4 Ezra has its basis in oral traditions that go back many generations before the author's day.

[16] Works such as the book of Jubilees, Enoch, the Apocalypse of Baruch, Wisdom of Solomon, and 4 Ezra all contain the doctrine of the renewal of creation (cf. Jub. 1.29; Enoch 45.4; 72.1; 2 Baruch 32.6; 44.12; 57.2; 4 Ezra 5.45; 7.75). Therefore, rather than an absolute negation of history, a number of apocalyptists envision world-regeneration. The doctrine of world-renewal is the direct teaching of Jesus (Mt. 19.28). This verse consists of the *ipsissima verba Jesu*. The 'new heavens' and 'new -earth' of Isaiah are, of course, echoed in 2 Pet. 3.13 and in Rev. 21.21.

[17] The dualism of the Two-Ages doctrine recognizes no continuity between the time of this world and of that which is to come: 'For behold, the days are coming when everything that has come into being will be given over to destruction, and it will be as if it had never been' (Baruch 31.5). Vielhauer, 'Apocalyptic', p. 588. Generally, at Qumran the new creation was not expected until the end of human history (1QS 4; 1QH 11). However, lQH 13 appears to be an exception: 'For thou hast shown them that which they had not (seen by removing all) ancient things and creating new ones, by breaking asunder things anciently established, and raising up the things of eternity'. Cf. Jubilees 1.29; 33.30, which indicate that the new age has already set in, but there is not a catastrophic breaking in the kingdom as in other apocalyptic writings; rather it is a gradual process.

into the divine realm. At Qumran the sectaries discerned a dualism that divides the whole cosmos between two hostile powers. In the War Rule, for example, Satan and his host are set against God and the Sons of Light. This struggle will not be resolved until the final destruction of evil on the day of judgment (1QM 1, 15-19).[18]

A basic religious conception of the Qumran Community was the doctrine of Two Spirits, one good and the other evil and respectively symbolized as Light and Darkness (1QS 3). The ethical antithesis is depicted in terms of a constant struggle of the angel of light and the angel of darkness for the souls of humanity. This is emphasized at some length in the War Rule where the 'Children of Light' find themselves in conflict with the 'Children of Darkness' in an apocalyptic war (1QM 1). The opposing forces divide the cosmos into two camps (1QS 3). To some extent, this cosmic rift is reflected within the individual and the community for good and evil. 'The nature of all the children is ruled by these (two spirits), and during their life all the host of men have a portion in their divisions and walk in (both) their ways' (1QS 4; cf. lQS 3).

Apocalyptic dualism may indicate recourse to Iranian thought where dualism is more absolute than in apocalypticism. It is a modified dualism that is seen within the framework of Hebrew monotheism. The Community Rule says, 'God has established two spirits in equal measure until the determined end' (1QS 4; cf. lQM 13). Both good and evil spirits are subject to God and have no independent existence. Too, God is the creator and Lord of both ages and will bring the present age to its end. Thus, apocalyptic avoids a radical metaphysical dualism by linking the Creator and his saving purpose to this age and the age to come.[19]

Determinism

Along with dualism, determinism is a prominent feature of Jewish apocalyptic. The apocalyptic writers believed that the entire course of history had been foreordained by God. Mainly from the view of

---

[18] To a great extent, this and other apocalyptic themes are brought out in the first column and the last five columns, the sections which Vermes thinks could be the primitive form of the War Rule. Much of the rest of the scroll is devoted to formal preparations and the proper formulations which appear on the banners and weapons.

[19] Vielhauer, 'Apocalyptic', p. 589; Betz, 'The Concept of Apocalyptic in the Theology of the Pannenberg Group', p. 202.

the schematization of history William R. Murdock traces the origin of the apocalyptic conception of history to Iranian thought and its determinism:

> The apocalyptic scheme represents the time divisions, the *Kairon taxeis*, within the predetermined limits of this present aeon. Apart from the fourfold schema (Dan. 2 and 7 and 2 Bar. 37-48), which derives from a non-Jewish source, and the sevenfold schema (1 En. 89.59; T. L. 16), which derives from Jeremiah (24.11-12), the apocalyptic schemata are also sevenfold or twelvefold. This fact sufficiently demonstrates that the apocalyptic schemata themselves derive from Iranian Babylonian syncretism and that the determinism presupposed by them is astrological determinism.[20]

Determinism is fundamental to the division of world history into periods. As well as duration and the number of periods the course of events is thought to be predetermined by God. But the movement of world history does not lead to progress; instead the world is growing progressively worse and evil will continue to increase until it has reached its limits and God intervenes to put an end to it. The author of 1 Enoch is extremely pessimistic: the historical order is moving toward an 'abyss' and a 'great destruction' (38.7).[21]

---

[20] William R. Murdock, 'History and Revelation in Jewish Apocalypticism', *Interpretation* 21 (1967), p. 169. There are numerous examples in apocalyptic literature of schematic periodizations of history and of calculations of the time of the *eschaton*. See 1 Enoch 52; 93.1-10; 2 Enoch 33; Testament of Abraham 17, 19, 20, 28; Testament of Levi; 2 Baruch 27, 56, 57. The schemes devised by the writers vary in estimations of the date of the end, the number and duration of the epochs. Some treat the period from the captivity of the end (2 Baruch 35-40); others survey longer periods (4 Ezra 14.11, 12). This phenomenon in apocalyptic books seeks to review and reinterpret history. The apocalyptists felt compelled to review past history in order to put the future in proper perspective. It is a methodology already introduced by the prophets (Ezek. 17.21-24).

[21] Cf. Russell, *The Method and Message of Jewish Apocalyptic*, p. 220. Apocalyptic writers see this aeon under the control of evil powers and in bondage to wickedness. Regardless of how good creation was originally, it has been turned aside from the divine purpose (4 Ezra 4.27; 8.1-3; 9.18-20; 2 Baruch 14.10-11; 21.19; 43.2; 74.2; 83.10-22; 1 Enoch 48.7; 2 Enoch 66.6). As a result of this and humanity's evil condition and moral failure the apocalyptists are pessimistic about salvation's arising out of this present aeon, but they are not skeptical about the ultimate future. Their hope was in the *eschaton* which would terminate the present historical order and inaugurate the new age. Consequently Vielhauer, 'Apocalyptic', p. 593, and Betz, 'The Concept of Apocalyptic in the Theology of the Pannenberg Group', pp. 201-202, rightly discern with William Murdock 'that apocalypticism does not want to write a "theology of history" in the sense of a salvation history'. In

That God has a fixed order of historical events is well attested in apocalyptic literature. Daniel states it thus: 'What is determined shall be done' (11.36).[22] This includes the outworking of divine wrath and a final judgment (5.24-28; 8.19; 9.26. Cf. 1 Enoch 84.4-6; lQS 4). In 2 Baruch 54.13 the purpose of God is seen in all: 'For with thy counsel Thou dost govern all the creatures … And thou hast established every fountain of light beside thee, and the treasures of wisdom beneath Thy throne hast Thou prepared' (cf. chap. 48). The Community Rule teaches that God has determined all that lies in the present and future (1QS 3). According to 4 Ezra the course and duration of the present world have been predetermined, and the decisive moment will soon arrive (4.33-50).[23] As for the length of this present age it is said that everything is counted, numbered, and pre-determined (Cf. 4.40-43). The end is imminent (Dan. 12.4-9; 1 Enoch 105.1; 4 Ezra 14.7-8).

Consequently, the conclusion may be drawn that the apocalyptists understand history from beginning to end to be determined by God. However, determinism in apocalyptic is not always seen as in accord with the divine will. 1 Enoch 83-90 is a survey of world history from Adam to the Messiah. This survey is depicted in terms of seventy periods to correspond with the rule of 'seventy shepherds' who are the angelic rulers of the heavenly bodies that determine the fate of Israel (89.59-60). As Murdock says, '… this determinism expresses a will that is contrary to God's will. For the "seventy shepherds" rebelled against God and brought undue suffering upon Israel (9:22ff.).'[24] Ultimately God was sovereign: 'And those seventy

---

schematizing history, the apocalyptists do not develop an outline of *Heilsgeschichte* that posits that the divine purpose is progressively realized in the present historical order but that the history of this age is a history of sin, an *Unheilsgeschichte*. Cf. Daniel 7; 1 Enoch 85-91; 2 Baruch 56-74. This does not mean that the scheme of the history of salvation has no place in apocalyptic thought. 4 Ezra 3.17-22 is a rehearsal of what God has done.

[22] Daniel may assume a fixed duration, but the details within the limits appear to be somewhat flexible. Natural elements of monotheistic faith are: divine control (12.21; 5.23), divine judgment (4.17, 24, 35; 5.25-26; 7.26), divine forgiveness (4.27; 9.16), and confidence in the above (2.28; 45). Other elements, however, reveal a trend toward determinism: time of fullness or completion (8.23; 9.2), numbered time (5.26; 8.14; 9.2, 24), appointed time or times (8.17, 19, 26; 9.27; 10.14; 11.27; 12.1, 9), and written judgment or fate (tablets of destiny, 10.21; 12.1).

[23] See also Robert A. Bartels, 'Law and Sin in 4th Edras and St. Paul', *Lutheran Quarterly* 1 (1949), p. 323.

[24] Murdock, 'History and Revelation in Jewish Apocalypticism', p. 170.

shepherds were judged and found guilty, and they were cast into that fiery abyss' (90.25).

Due to the presence of evil, God's almighty hand was more clearly seen in events of the remote past and will be seen in the future; but though God was understood to be in control, his reign in the present was obscured by the presence of evil. This was only for the duration of the present world order. God had ordained the time of judgment when he would destroy all evil.

The Urzeit-Endzeit Motif

As well as formulating schematizations of history, apocalyptic proposes that the principle of *Urzeit* plays an important role in eschatological development. The 'Endzeit' is equal to the 'Urzeit';[25] the last stage will reproduce the first; the new age restores conditions as they were at the beginning of history.[26] The viewing of history on the basis of primordialty is what Ernst Käsemann refers to as the 'apocalyptic principle'.[27] Volz calls attention to the fact that there are two *Urzeiten* in apocalyptic thought. The principle anticipates that the end will correspond to the beginning and sees the *Urzeit* either as creation and beginning of humankind or as Israel and the beginning of the people of God. The former stresses a universal eschatological perspective; the latter a national eschatology.[28]

First, we shall consider the principle in terms of the *Endzeit*, the new creation, corresponding with the *Urzeit*, the first creation.[29] At the *Endzeit* the second creation is seen as a renewal of the old creation (2 Baruch 32.6; Jub. 1.29; 4 Ezra 7.25), a transformation or change of the old world (1 Enoch 45.4, 5; 2 Baruch 49.3-4; 4 Ezra 6.16) and a replacement of the first creation (1 Enoch 72.1).[30] The new creation will be preceded by primeval silence as original creation (4 Ezra 7.30) and is portrayed as a reversal of the work of Adam (4 Ezra 7.119-26;

---

[25] R.H. Charles, *The Ascension of Isaiah* (London: Society for Promoting Christian Knowledge, 1917), p. xviii.

[26] This idea is stated in the Old Testament (Isa. 11.6-8; Ezek. 34.25-27).

[27] Käsemann, 'The Beginnings of Christian Theology', p. 33.

[28] Volz, *Die Eschatologie der judischen Gemeinde im neutestamentlichen Zeitalter*, pp. 113, 359.

[29] Russell, *The Method and Message of Jewish Apocalyptic*, p. 282, concedes that the *Urzeit* principle defies a simple analysis. He cites N.A. Dahl's analysis that sees the correlation of the end with the beginning in seven ways.

[30] Cf. 1 Enoch 45.4; 91.15, 16; Isa. 5.7, 66.22; Rev. 21.1. Noteworthy is that in 1 Enoch 91.16 there is reference to a new heaven but not to a new earth.

8.51-54; 2 Baruch 56.6). The curse, the consequence of the sin of Adam and Eve, will be removed in the new world (2 Baruch 73.5-7) and paradisaical conditions restored:[31] the Tree of Life and longevity (1 Enoch 10.18-22) and primeval fruitfulness and fertility (1 Enoch 10.18-22). For Israel it will be a time of miraculous fruitfulness (Joel 2.19; 3.18; cf. Amos 9.13). After a period of battle against Beliar and the evil spirits the closed gates to paradise in the Garden of Eden will be open again and 'the threatening sword' removed (Test. Levi 18.10; cf. 4 Ezra 8.52). Contrary to the original garden in this paradise the fruit will endure uncorrupted (4 Ezra 7.123), and the inhabitants of the new creation will return to the primitive righteousness of Eden (1 Enoch 90.38-39).

Furthermore, apocalyptic hope that has the national eschatology in view expects that the *Endzeit* will correlate with the creation of the nation of Israel, that is, the *Urzeit* that began with Abraham (2 Baruch 57.1) and continued through the time of Moses and the announcement of the law at Sinai (59.1-2). The history of this age is said to be no longer than 'From Abraham to Abraham', that is, from Abraham to an immediate offspring (4 Ezra 6.8). In the time of Abraham, Isaac, and Jacob the unwritten law was obeyed and hoped for the new age renewed (57.1-2).

Spiritual transformation is expected at the end-time that is to parallel the period from Abraham to Moses. This is to be accomplished by the renewed study of the law given to Moses (Jub. 23.26-27). Still another factor is the comparison of final Exodus with the original

---

[31] Hermann Strack and Paul Billerbeck, *Kommentar zum Neuen Testament aus Talmud und Midrasch* III (Munchen: C.H. Beck'sche Verlagsbuchhandlung, 1926), pp. 247-54, lists six blessings that Man was supposed to have lost as a result of his Fall: (1) 'the glow of his face'; (2) 'the length of his life'; (3) 'the height of his stature'; (4) 'the fertility of the earth'; (5) 'the fruitfulness of the trees'; and (6) 'the brilliance of the celestial bodies'. Note that the first three involve humanity directly; the last three are directed against creation. These six blessings were to be restored to humanity by the coming Messiah. In addition, he would bring with him ten further blessings for humanity:

> the radiance of the stars will be increased: living water healing all infirmities will flow; the trees will bear fruits every month; the destroyed cities will be rebuilt; Jerusalem will be built up out of sapphire; peace will reign among the Israelites; Israel will enjoy peace with the animal kingdom also; tears and complaints will cease; there will be no more death; sighing, cries of anguish, and groaning will no longer be heard.

The implication is that the Messiah's coming would have cosmic significance, capable of restoring the original condition of creation.

Exodus. The ten tribes of the Northern Kingdom are to return from the dispersion to Palestine; and the river of Euphrates is to open before them, as did the Red Sea when Israel went out of Egypt (4 Ezra 13.40-41). Again Mt. Sinai is to be a place where special revelation is given (4 Ezra 14.1-17). God is to appear once more at Sinai (1 Enoch 1. Lt) and manna is to be restored as food (2 Baruch 29.8).

The apocalyptists understand that each of the primeval periods ended on account of sin. The *Urzeit* that dates from the original creation was ended by Adam's sin (Jub. 5.1-2; 4 Ezra 3.4-10; cf. Wisd. of Sol. 10.1-2). The *Urzeit* that had its inception with Abraham was brought to its end in Moses' day by the incident of the Golden Calf (1 Enoch 89.31).

Consequently, apocalyptic with its over-arching principle of *Endzeit gleich Urzeit* appeals to the *Urzeit* as the basis of hope rather than to God's continuous saving acts, beginning with the patriarchs and continuing throughout the history of Israel to the present.[32]

Angelic and Demonic Powers
Apocalyptic literature assigns a significant role to angels and demons. This is seen in both Daniel and Zechariah. The Book of Jubilees and the Testaments of the Twelve Patriarchs develop the idea further.[33] The problem of moral evil, of which human suffering is only part, gave rise in a number of post-exilic writings to the notion that the angels to whom God had given authority over the nations[34] and the physical universe rebelled against God and took power into their own hands. Thus those "tendencies toward evil" which appear in the biblical references to "the Satan" and his legions are presented as

---

[32] von Rad, *Old Testament Theology*, II, pp. 303-304, notes the lack of interest on the part of apocalyptists in *Heilsgeschichte* and that their surveys of the history of Israel are designed to place in historical perspective the present generation of Jews and their circumstance. Von Rad overstates the case in denying that apocalyptic literature has an existential relation to history, but the apocalyptists did place their predictions within a historical context in an effort to legitimize their predictions. Historical notes are interspersed throughout the visions of 4 Ezra 3-16, but in the main they lend an air of validity to the apocalyptic predictions. Other examples are 1 Enoch 85-90, 2 Baruch 56.1-74.4 and Assumption of Moses 2-6.

[33] Cf. Test. Of Dan. 2-6; Test. Of Reuben 3.1-6; Jub. 2, 4, 5, 15 where the world of spirits is divided into classes and functions.

[34] Jubilees 15.31-32 states that spirits were placed over all nations to lead them astray except Israel, which is alone ruled by the Lord.

archenemies of God, bent on controlling and so ultimately destroying not only the human race but even the cosmos itself.'[35]

Fallen Angels and Origin of Evil

A remarkable feature is the prominent place given to demons in connection with evil, particularly its origin. With the story of Gen. 6.1-2 as a backdrop 1 Enoch 6.26, for example, describes how angels, the Watchers, saw the beautiful daughters of men and said, 'Come, let us choose us wives from among the children of man and beget children (6.2)'. Under Semjaza, their leader, they descended to the earth and carried out their plan. The offsprings of the angels and their wives were 'great giants'. The giants began to devour men and one another after they had eaten all that was edible (7.4-6). When the giants died their spirits became demons, oppressing men and causing trouble and destruction on the earth (15.11). These evil spirits, according to this writer, continue their malignant activities until the final judgment (16.1).

A somewhat different version is given in the Book of Jubilees where Noah prays that God will abolish from off the earth the evil spirits, the offsprings of the Watchers (10.3). God commanded that all the evil spirits be bound in the place of condemnation. At the request of their chief, Mastema, nine parts of them were bound but the tenth part remained on the earth subject to Satan (19.7-11).[36] While these evil spirits were precluded from hurting Noah's sons (10.13), they encourage humans to make molten images, to worship idols, and 'to do all manner of wrong and sin', including war and bloodshed (11.4-5.). Thus, the Book of Enoch and the Book of Jubilees make it clear that evil comes from fallen spirits. Their area of activities is by the permission of God, but humans are held responsible since they allowed themselves to be seduced to sin by the fallen angels (1 Enoch 8.1-4) and have corrupted their ways and thoughts (Jub. 5.2-3.).[37]

---

[35] Russell, *The Method and Message of Jewish Apocalyptic*, p. 238.

[36] 'Tenth' is a modification of the version of 1 Enoch 15, 16.

[37] In addition to a strong interest in tracing the origin of evil back to the rebellion or fall of the angels a number of apocalyptic writers find in the paradise story of Genesis 3 a historical explanation of it. This is reflected in the theology of 2 Baruch. The author accepts Genesis 3 as the account of humanity's fall into sin (48.42, 43) and teaches that Adam's transgression is universal in effect (18.1, 2; 17.3, 4; 19.8; 23.4; 48.42-50; 54.15; 56.6). In Jub. 3.17-35 and Test. Of Levi 18.10, 11 this appears side by side with the Watcher's explanation.

The view that humans are responsible for their sin is commonly held. They retain free will in spite of Adam's fall (Jub. 54.15-19) and have freedom to choose between right and wrong (19.1-3). The choice of evil on the part of humans is deliberate (51.16). 'Adam is therefore not the cause, save only his own soul, but each one of us has been the adam of his own soul' (2 Baruch 54.19; cf. 17.3; 23.4).

Whether traced to the paradise story of Genesis 3 or to the Watchers of Gen. 6.1-2 or stated in terms of Adam's transgression or the transgressions of his descendants, evil is understood by apocalyptic writers to be cosmic, demonic power that has influenced humanity.

Anti-God Figures

Two anti-God figures, Satan and Beliar, are prominent in apocalyptic theology.

Satan

Apocalyptic literature presents divergent accounts of Satan[38] and his activities. The parables of Enoch (37-71) speak of Satans who existed in heaven before the fall of angels and who were held responsible for that event. Phanuel is represented as 'Fending off Satans' and forbidding them to come before the Lord of Spirits to accuse them who dwell on the earth (40.7). In 69.4-12, 24 a list of five Satans, whose activities are described, is given. The first and the second are said to have been responsible for leading astray the angels and for bringing them down to earth where they sinned with the 'daughters of men' (69.4). The third Satan brought about the fall of Eve (69.6). This class of Satans is presented as ruled by the chief Satan (53.3; 54.6). So, there is a host of Satans with one Satan as the leader.[39]

The Testaments of the Twelve Patriarchs contain scattered references to Satan. The spirit of wrath, it is said, 'goeth always with lying at the right hand of Satan' (Test. Dan 3.6). Satan is declared to be the prince of Dan (Test. Dan 5.6) and the patriarch Dan also urges his sons to beware of the spirits of Satan and his spirits (6.1). The spirit

---

[38] The Old Testament contains the first small beginnings of the stream of Hebrew thought concerning Satan as God's opponent. 'Satan' becomes the official title of a distinct personality in four passages, namely Zech. 3.1; Job 1 and 2 and 1 Chron. 21.1. In 1 Chron. 21.1 the name Satan appears for the first time without an article and thus becomes a proper name.

[39] The terms Satan and Devil are used interchangeably in the Books of Adam and Eve.

of hatred works together with Satan (Test. Gad 4.7), and humans at death show their righteousness or unrighteousness 'when they meet the angels of the Lord and of Satan' (Test. Asher 6.4).[40]

Beliar (Belial)

A further development of the anti-God figure centers on the figure of Beliar.[41] In the third book of the Sibylline oracles 63-92, Beliar is depicted as one who is to come in the later time and as a miracle worker who will deceive faithful Hebrews. In places he is represented as a spiritual force working against God, and his function is 'to accuse' people before God (Jub. 1.20).

The Testaments of the Twelve Patriarchs abound in references to Beliar as an anti-God figure to appear in the last time (Test. Issachar 6.1). Fornication, it is said, brings humans into derision with Beliar. If fornication does not overcome the mind, Beliar cannot overcome the human (Test. Reuben 4.7, 11). Beliar is called, 'the prince of deceit' (Test. Simon 2.7). The works of Beliar are opposed to 'the law of the Lord' (Test. Levi 19.1). Beliar rules over the soul (Test. Dan 4.7); but if humans do righteousness and love the Lord, every spirit of Beliar will flee from them (Test. Issachar 7.7). The reference to the 'Spirits of Beliar' in some of the passages show that Beliar is regarded as the chief of evil spirits like Satan (Test. Dan 1.7). A prominent function assigned to Beliar and his spirits in the Testaments is that of tempting humans. This function is also a characteristic of Satan.

Likewise, the anti-God figure Beliar is prominent in the literature of Qumran. According to the Community Rule the novices at the time of initiation must swear 'not to turn away from Him through any fear or terror or through any trial to which they may be subjected

---

[40] There are other demonic figures in this body of literature whose activities are similar to those of Satan. Azazel, who in the Old Testament is conceived as a demon of the desert is portrayed in 1 Enoch 1-15 as one of the principal leaders of the angels who descended to the earth and intermarried with woman. Samjaza is described by 1 Enoch as one of the fallen angels and with Azazel is the chief of those angels (chapter 6). There are references to two mythical monsters, Leviathan and Behemoth, as God's opponents (1 Enoch 60.7-10; 4 Ezra 6.49-52). In the book of Enoch the Medes and the Persians are bring stirred by the 'Nephilim' to evil and to war against 'the land of his elect ones', that is, Palestine (Enoch 56.5-8). For Enoch these nations are the kingdom of God and Magog which we find in the book of Ezekiel (38-39).

[41] There are no references to Beliar in the Old Testament, but in 2 Cor. 6.15 we do find a reference.

through the dominion of Belial' (1QS 1).[42] The people of the community thought that they were living perpetually in the 'day of Belial' (1 QS 2) and the people of the world were divided into the Sons of Light and Sons of Darkness. In the hands of the Prince of Light is the dominion over all Sons of Righteousness, while the Angel of Darkness has dominion over the Sons of Perversion. This conception of the anti-God figure is depicted by the War Rule in the eschatological war between 'the Sons of Light' and the 'Sons of Darkness' (1QM 1.1-2). We are not concerned with the details of the war. The author of the War Rule believes that the war will last forty years, and the Sons of Light will be finally victorious after they shall have suffered many defeats. It is not easy to say definitely whether the reference is to political or spiritual warfare. There are names of nations mentioned while at the same time Beliar is said to be at the head of the army. Beliar may, therefore, be identified with the power that oppressed the community since a political enemy was also the religious enemy of the community.[43]

Our investigation indicates that the activities of Beliar are similar to those of Satan. The Martyrdom of Isaiah seems to make no distinction between Satan and Beliar. In this work we have references to three princes of evil – Beliar, Sammael, and Satan – and it is difficult to determine any differences among them (1.8; 2.1, 4). Similar functions are ascribed to all of them. It is said that Sammael will serve Manasseh who will also become a follower of Belial (1.8). Both Sammael and Beliar are said to dwell in Manasseh (2.1; 1.8; 3.11). As a result of Sammael's abiding in Manasseh, he served Satan and his angels (2.2). In 2.4 Beliar is declared as the ruler of the world. The phrase 'Satan and his angels and his powers' (2.2) appears to be a parallel conception to Beliar 'the angel of lawlessness' (2.4).

This research does very little to show what specific relations exist between Beliar and Satan. Both Beliar and Satan are supernatural spirits and are mentioned as God's opponents and as the leaders of other spirits. Their activities as tempters and seducers are identical and they are depicted as destroyers of God's creation. We can conclude with Langton that the 'presentation of the relations of the

---

[42] See Theodor H. Gaster, *The Dead Sea Scrolls* (New York: Doubleday & Company, 1956).

[43] Volz, *Die Eschatologie der jüdischen Gemeinde im neutestamentlichen Zeitalter*, p. 77, points out instances of renegade Jews who were designated as 'sons of Belial'.

three powers of evil is no doubt largely due to the fact that these parallel conceptions prevailed at the same time, and no definite ideas existed as to their relations to each other'.[44] Beliar may be identical with Satan.

Messianic Expectation

Pivotal to Jewish eschatology was the messianic hope.[45] This expectation in the prophets was an earthly and horizontal one. Several apocalyptic writers presupposed a messianic era in which God's rule would be established on the earth. This would be the result of a series of eschatological events. Usually the era is thought to be temporary and to be a time of transition into the 'age to come' in which the righteous would enjoy eternal bliss and perfection either on the earth or in heaven. This section is devoted to events that are expected to occur in the messianic era.

The Messiah and Messianic Kingdom

The messianic concept varies considerably from one apocalyptic writer to another,[46] but the person of the Messiah is one aspect of messianic expectation which permeates several apocalyptic writings. This is seen in the Book of Daniel. The author of the book directs the attention of the people from the earthly kingdoms to someone supernatural, who can deliver the people. The earthly kingdoms are to be destroyed. This is clearly illustrated by the vision of the four beasts. The beasts represent the four kingdoms, and when these are taken away the scene of the vision continues with the appearance of one like a son of man before the Ancient of Days and to him is given an everlasting dominion (7.13, 14). The interpretation of the vision is that after the earthly kingdoms are ended, 'the saints of the Most High shall receive the kingdom for ever, for ever and ever' (v. 18).

---

[44] Edward Langton, *Essentials of Demonology* (London: Epworth Press, 1949), p. 139.

[45] The messianic expectation in the Old Testament goes back to the beginning of the monarchy in Israel (1 Samuel 8, 9, 10). Schoeps, *Paul: Theology of the Apostle in Light of Jewish Religious History*, pp. 92-93, notes that in the messianic expectation of the prophets the Messiah was not viewed as a person with supernatural power but as an executive officer of God. The exile intensified the messianic hope. While the messianic expectation in the Old Testament was that of a final age, it is a new aeon of this world's history that is expected, not the end of history.

[46] A messianic concept is at best vague in the book of Jubilees. Jubilees 31.18 intimates that a Messiah would arise from the tribe of Judah, but his function would seem to be somewhat subordinate to the priestly house of Levi.

The supernatural figure who is to possess the kingdom is 'a son man.'[47] This figure is very prominent in the apocalyptic writings, especially in the book of 1 Enoch 37-71 and 4 Ezra. In 1 Enoch the Son of Man is named before the Ancient of Days (48.2, 3), thus suggesting that the Messiah existed with God from the beginning. Other names are given to the Messiah in the apocalyptic books, such as 'the Righteous One' (Enoch 38.2), 'the Elect One' (1 Enoch 52.4), and 'My Son' (4 Ezra 7.28). He is described as having compassion, mercifulness, and righteousness in ruling his people and as walking in meekness and righteousness with humanity. No sin was found in him (Test. Judah 24.1, 2). The Messiah is divine, pre-existent, and immortal (4 Ezra 12.32-33; 14.9-10) yet purely human (12.32).

Generally, a messianic prince is expected; nevertheless, the Messiah is not indispensable to the eschatological kingdom.[48] Some writers see no need for a human Messiah,[49] whereas according to others the Messiah or some other figure serving as God's emissary plays a prominent role. For instance, in 1 Enoch the Messiah is the Judge (chap. 45) though usually in apocalyptic literature God is portrayed as Judge. At the time of judgment God will set him on a throne of glory (55.4), even on His own throne (15.3; 61.8; 69.29); and he will judge both men and angels (61.9). He shall judge even the 'secret things' (55.4). The author of 1 Enoch mentions the different ways in which the enemies of God will meet their fate on the last day. Suddenly, the Head of the Days will appear, and with him the Son of Man (46.2-4; 48.2), to execute judgment. The fallen angels are cast into a fiery furnace (54.6); the kings and the mighty are given into the hands of the righteous (38.5) and their destruction furnishes a spectacle to the righteous as they burn and vanish forever out of sight (48.9; 62.12), to be tortured in Gehenna by the angels of punishment (53.3-5; 54.1, 2). The remaining sinners and the godless people are driven from the face of the earth (38.3; 4.12; 45.6). The Son of Man slays them with the word of his mouth (62.2).

The Messiah is portrayed as possessing great power. He is to war against Beliar and the powers of wickedness (Test. Reub. 6.12; Test. Levi 18.2; Test. Dan 5.10) and give the faithful power to tread

---

[47] The identification of the 'Son of Man' has been a perennial problem for biblical scholars.
[48] Russell, *The Method and Message of Jewish Apocalyptic*, p. 309.
[49] Russell, *The Method and Message of Jewish Apocalyptic*, p. 309.

upon evil spirits and bind Beliar (Test. Levi 18.12), who is to be cast in the fire (Test. Judges 25.3). Moreover, he is to destroy the evil power of Beliar and restore the kingdom (Test. Zeb. 9.8). At the time of the resurrection he will choose the righteous and holy and bring them to salvation (1 Enoch 51.1-3). In 4 Ezra he is the Savior of the world (13.25-26).

Political success of the Messiah is emphasized. There was a growing consciousness among the Jews that one of the tasks of the Messiah would be the destruction of those nations oppressing them (2 Baruch 72.2-6). A significant passage which summarizes the messianic beliefs of the Qumran Community occurs in the Blessings where the Messiah is depicted as a political ruler who will destroy the nations and the wicked with the breath of his mouth. The references to him as the Lion of Judah and the Scepter of rulers anticipate that he will be a Davidic Warrior Messiah (1Q5b 5).[50]

The Kingdom of the Messiah envisions a 'new community' which is liberated from the total misery of human society and a kingdom of 'peace', 'joy', and 'freedom' (2 Baruch 71.2; 72.2-74.4). In apocalyptic, the messianic kingdom is the transformation of history on earth (1 Enoch 45.3-5; Jub. 1.29). A marked difference between the messianic expectation in the apocalyptic writings and that of the prophets is the fact that in the latter the messianic kingdom was generally pictured as eternal on earth.[51] But in the apocalyptic writings the messianic age was a transition to the next age, known as 'the world to come'. The order is 'This World', 'the Messianic Age', and the 'World to Come'. With the advent of the Messiah the messianic age, the heavenly Jerusalem, will come down to earth. The final judgment is the end of this world and the beginning 'the World to Come'. After the final judgment will come the 'new world' (2 Baruch 44.12; 4 Ezra 7.112-14).

---

[50] The person and character of the Messiah are subject to varying opinions among the scholars. The Damascus Rule alludes to two Messiahs: 'the messiah out of Aaron and Israel'. This phrase could refer to the Messianic King and the Prophet who were expected by the sectaries. There have been attempts to identify the mysterious figure of the 'teacher of Righteousness' as the Messiah. It is also not clear whether the Messiah from Aaron is the same as the one from Israel or different.

[51] The only exception to this is in Isa. 65.17 and 66.22, where the prophet speaks of a 'new heaven and a new earth'.

Messianic Woes ('Birth Pangs')[52]

A prominent feature of apocalyptic expectation was that the coming of the Messiah is to be preceded by terrors, tumults, and chaos. Such catastrophes are described in the Old Testament. These are commonly found in connection with expressions like the 'day of the Lord', 'the day', and 'that day' and are expected to precede an eschatological advent of Yahweh (cf. Amos 5.16, 17; 6.11; 8.10; 8.11, 12; Joel 1-2; Zeph. 1.14-16; Isa. 13.9, 10).[53] The apocalyptic portrayal of the 'day of the Lord' reveals essentially the same characteristics of the prophetic day of the Lord: imminence, universality, and judgment (cf. 4 Ezra 7.37-38; Jub. 23.11-12; 24.30-31; 2 Baruch 55.6-7). 'Sometimes the coming of this great Day is the result of the direct intervention of God himself; at other times he acts through his chosen Messiah who establishes his kingdom upon the earth.'[54] Our concern here is the signs and portents of Jewish apocalyptic that herald the triumphal advent of the Messiah or Yahweh and that precede the end. The investigation will be carried on under three headings: signs in nature, struggle among nations, and religious apostasy.

Signs in Nature

Less prominence is given to messianic woes in the Old Testament than in later apocalyptic thought, but they are not altogether lacking. In genuine apocalyptic style Joel expects great changes for the worse in all of nature. He anticipates that the 'day of the Lord' will be preceded by a plague of locusts that causes failure in the production of cereals and fruits (chap. 1). He goes on to portray that day as 'a day of darkness and gloom of clouds and thick darkness' and on it 'all of the inhabitants of the land tremble' (2.1-2; cf. Isa. 24.17-23; Zeph. 1.14-16). Just as the cosmic signs of earthquakes and eclipse of sun, moon, and stars picture God as entering into judgment with the nations of the earth (2.10-11), so also in 3.15, 16 the same signs are used to picture God in the act of saving Israel. Zechariah 14.4 and Ezek. 38.20 see earthquakes as a sign of the end.

---

[52] The technical term for messianic woes is *hebhle di Mashiah*. The Greek ὠδῖνες is the term for birthpangs and links up with the idea of messianic woes.

[53] The eighth-century prophets and others after them, challenged the popular thought that the day of the Lord would mean salvation for Israel and destruction for her enemies.

[54] Russell, *The Method and Message of Jewish Apocalyptic*, p. 272.

The portents in heaven have impressive parallels in extra-canonical apocalyptic literature: 'And the moon shall alter her order, and not appear at her time. And in those days the sun shall be seen, and he shall journey in the evening.' (1 Enoch 80.4, 5). 'The sun shall suddenly shine forth at night, and the moon by day ... and the stars shall change' (4 Ezra 5.4, 5). In the third book of the Sibylline Oracles 77-92 the apocalyptist envisions before the advent of the Messiah a total disruption of the order of nature and a great conflagration that burns up even the sea.[55]

Struggle Among People and Nations

Strife and wars also proclaim the nearness of the end. Ezekiel predicts a complete break-up of the family: 'every man's sword will be against his brother' and there will be bloodshed (38.21-22; cf. Mk 13.7-8). The rise of kingdom after kingdom is an end-time expectation in Dan. 7.3-4 where the four beasts represent four kingdoms. Each kingdom is overthrown and succeeded as a world power by another. Essentially the same expectation is found in 4 Ezra chapters 11 and 12. The author records a vision of the eagle that appeared from the sea. God reveals to him the interpretation that the eagle represents the fourth kingdom of Daniel 7. After this kingdom shall appear a series of kingdoms one after the other, until all the kingdoms are destroyed. At the end of all this is the appearance of a lion who is interpreted to be 'the Messiah who the Most High hath kept unto the end of the day' (12.32).

As well as the rise of one kingdom after the other, the order of the day is wars and hatred among people and nations. All nations are summoned to arm themselves for a great battle and to march to the valley where it will be fought (Joel 2.9-12a).[56] It appears also in 4 Ezra 13.5, 33-34, 'an innumerable multitude of men were gathered together from the four winds of heaven to make war ...', 'an innumerable multitude desiring to come and conquer' (cf. 1 Enoch 56.5-6, cf. 2 Baruch 70.2, 3, 6). After these events 'the Most High will reveal

---

[55] Cf. Assumption of Moses 10.3-5, 1QH 5 and apocalyptic passages in the Synoptic Gospels – Mk 13.24; Mt. 24.29; Lk. 21.11. There is basis for describing such woes as stages in 'uncreation'. In the book of Revelation, the woes that are depicted are the reverse of the order of creation and may be described as the 'uncreation' of the world. I am indebted to Eugene S. Wehrli for this observation.

[56] Cf. also Ezek. 38, 39; Rev. 16.16, 1QM 1 for the final eschatological struggle between good and evil.

those people whom He has prepared' (20.7), so that they may wage war with the enemies.

Religious Apostasy

Increasing wickedness and religious rebellion is still another sign that precedes the end. The author of 4 Ezra warns his contemporaries that the ways of truth shall be hidden, and iniquity shall increase beyond what they had seen or heard (5.1, 2; cf. Jub. 23.14-23; 1 Enoch 91.7; Assumption of Moses 5.4; CDC 1, 5, 8; 1 QpHab. 2).[57] Along with faithlessness, the anti-God[58] is to appear and lead many away from God. This is mentioned in the Third Book of Sibylline Oracles (63-70).[59]

A rather consistent feature of the apocalyptist is the shortening of the 'latter days'. Generally, this is in the interest of preserving the elect (1 Baruch 10.1, 2; 54.1; Mk 13.20; Mt. 24.22). Nevertheless, the troubles that befall the nation of Israel were understood to be not only natural catastrophes but also a prelude to the coming of the messianic kingdom and the Messiah.

Cosmic Transformation

A number of apocalyptic authors envision changes in the world as a whole during the establishment of the messianic kingdom. Typical is the depiction in the book of Jubilees of the world renewal that is expected to occur

> when the heavens, and the earth shall be renewed and all their creation according to the powers of the heaven, and according to all creation of the earth until the sanctuary of the Lord shall be made in Jerusalem on Mount Zion and all the luminaries be renewed for all healing and for peace and for blessing for all the

---

[57] The Third Hymn from Qumran is full of expressions that are indicative of messianic woes. The increase of evil is stressed in such statements: 'All the snares of the pit were open, and the lures of wickedness were set up … the torrents of Satan shall reach to all sides of the world.'

[58] In the Old Testament the anti-God idea can be traced back to Ezekiel 38-39 where Gog is the leader of the forces set in opposition to God. See Russell, *The Method and Message of Jewish Apocalyptic*, p. 276.

[59] See also Dan. 11.30-31 As a reference to Antiochus Epiphanes, Daniel speaks of the anti-God's profaning the temple (cf. 1 Macc. 1.20-23) and exalting himself above every god. The concept of the temple is important in apocalyptic. According to 1 Enoch 91.13 and Jub. 1.17, a renewed or new temple will be established in the last days.

elect of Israel (1.29; cf. 1 Enoch 45.4; 72.1; 2 Baruch 32.6; 44.12; 57.2).[60]

The same author expects that 'in the new creation' beginning with the Garden of Eden 'the earth will be sanctified from all its guilt and its uncleanness throughout the generations of the world' (4.26) and that in those days 'men live in peace and in joy', for there will be no Satan or any evil destroyer (23.29; cf. Assumption of Moses 10.1). Though the sectaries at Qumran held to varying eschatological beliefs, they were convinced, too, that the fulfillment of God's purpose for them and the world was in the future. In some instances, final consummation is depicted in terms of a cosmic war in which evil is decisively put down (1QH 3, 6; 1Qm 1, 2), but other references forecast eschatological renewal of both man and the world (1QS 4; 1QH 11, 13).[61]

The changes that are anticipated in the messianic era do not apply in all instances to the created world as a whole. There are passages which envision the transformation of humankind. For example, when the Messiah is established on his throne, 2 Baruch 73.2-4 forecasts communal renewal:

> And then healing shall descend in dew, and disease shall withdraw, and anxiety and anguish and lamentation pass from amongst men … and no one shall die untimely, nor shall any adversity suddenly befall and judgments, and revilings, and contentions, and revenges, and blood, and passions, and envy, and hatred, and whatsoever things are like these shall go into condemnation when they are removed.

Often moral and spiritual renewal is stated in terms of the removal of all that is the opposite of righteousness (1 Enoch 91.8; 107.1).

---

[60] Charles, *The Apocrapha and Pseudepigrapha of the Old Testament*, II, p. 13, observes that Jubilees 1.29 and Test. Levi 18 teach a gradual transformation of the world, moral and physical. This view was replaced by the expectation of a violent revolution of things (1 Enoch 91.16; 45.4; 2 Baruch 32.6; 4 Ezra 7.75). But it is not always clear whether transformation is seen as an instantaneous event or a gradual process (1 Enoch 45.4).

[61] The writer of 1QH 13 might have believed that in his day the cosmic process was under way: 'For thou hast shown them that which they have not seen by removing all ancient things creating new ones, by breaking asunder things anciently established and raising up the things of eternity'.

Still another anticipated change in the messianic age is the transformation of the righteous. Here two passages from 1 Enoch are apt: 'And the righteous shall have been clothed with garments of glory, and these shall be the garments of life from the Lord of Spirits' (62.15, 16). 'I will transform those who are born in darkness, who in the flesh were not recompensed with such honour as their faithfulness deserved. And I will bring forth in shining light those who have loved My holy name … And they shall be resplendent …' (108.11-13). This subject will be further examined in connection with the hope of resurrection of the dead.

The Resurrection

It was in apocalyptic thought that the hope of the resurrection of the individual dead was introduced into Jewish eschatology.[62] In the Old Testament, Isa. 26.19 is the beginning of resurrection theology:[63] 'Thy dead shall live and their bodies shall rise.' Apparently, this does not envision a universal resurrection. According to 26.14a, there is no resurrection of the dead rulers: 'They are dead, they will not live; they are shades, they will not rise'. An extension of the resurrection appears in Daniel 12.2-3:

> And many of those who sleep in the dust of the earth shall awake, some to everlasting life, and some to shame and everlasting contempt. And those who are wise shall shine like the brightness of firmament; and those who turn many to righteousness, like the stars forever and ever (12.2-3).

The added dimension here is the condemnation of 'some to shame and everlasting contempt'. The statement 'many' shall awake raises the question whether the reference is to a universal resurrection. If this refers to the resurrection only of the best and worst, universal resurrection was a belief that still lay in the future.

---

[62] According to Charles, *Eschatology*, p. 130, the eschatology of the prophets dealt only with the destiny of the nation, but the apocalyptic doctrine of the resurrection was a synthesis of national and individual eschatology. Charles thinks that the synthesis was due to the connecting of the doctrine of immortality of the faithful with that of the coming messianic kingdom.

[63] The question of the origin of the Jewish doctrine of the resurrection is interlocked with the date of Isaiah 24-27, since it is thought that these chapters contain the first reference to the resurrection in Jewish writings. See T. Francis Glasson, *Greek Influence in Jewish Eschatology* (London: SPCK, 1961), p. 31.

The idea of the resurrection of the dead as an aspect of messianism is reinforced in 2 Baruch and 4 Ezra.[64] The New World is described as the world to which there is no end and is believed to bring death to an end (2 Baruch 21.23). 'And the earth shall restore those that sleep in her and the dust those that are at rest therein' (4 Ezra 7.32). Both 2 Baruch and 4 Ezra reflect the belief in the resurrection of all men (cf. Test. of Benj. 10.6-8; 1 Enoch 51.1-2).

Nevertheless, there are apocalyptic writers who make no mention of the resurrection of the wicked (Psa. of Sol. 3.16). In 1 Enoch 83-90 and 2 Enoch reference is made to the resurrection of the righteous only. The implication of 1 Enoch 90.33 is that the righteous alone will rise to share in the kingdom. We are told that following their resurrection the righteous will be transformed into the likeness of the Messiah who is represented as a white bull: 'And I (Enoch) saw till all their generations were transformed and they all became white bulls' (v. 37). Too, 2 Enoch envisions no resurrection of the unrighteous. The righteous dead rise. It is not as in the above reference a resurrection of the flesh. They rise in possession of 'spiritual' bodies that befit life in a heavenly paradise (8.5; 65.10).[65]

A number of apocalyptists make a distinction between 'physical' and 'spiritual' bodies and teach that the righteous will be gloriously transformed when they are raised from the dead. This is illustrated in 1 Enoch. The righteous are to rise from the earth and are to be clothed with garments of glory and life that will not grow old (62.15, 16). Their physical bodies are to be 'resplendent' and dwell in 'shining light' (108.11-12). 2 Baruch insists that both the wicked and the righteous will be raised. The dead will be raised exactly as they were when they died (cf. Sib. Oracles 4.180-81) and will be able to recognize one another. After the judgment, which immediately follows the resurrection, the bodies will be changed either to one more glorious or to one

---

[64] The hope of the resurrection of the dead is typical of apocalyptic writings, but in a few apocalyptic books no reference is made to the resurrection. In the Book of Jubilees, the resurrection of the body is not explicitly found. The righteous will see their vindication; but then 'their bones will rest in the earth and their spirits will have much joy' (23.31). The writer apparently was influenced by the Hellenistic idea of the immortality of the soul. See Russell, *The Method and Message of Jewish Apocalyptic*, p. 372, for additional references to the doctrine of the immortality of the soul in apocalyptic books.

[65] See Russell, *The Method and Message of Jewish Apocalyptic*, p. 370.

worse (50.1-51.2).[66] The righteous 'shall be made like the angels' and 'changed from light into the splendor of glory' (51.10).

Consequently, in a number of places the 'spiritual body' is the counterpart to the 'physical body'[67] and is described as a 'glorious body'. Little is said about the specific properties of this 'glorious body', but it is frequently represented in terms of a transformed physical body.[68] According to Russell, the nature of the resurrection body corresponds with the nature of the kingdom that is expected to be the lot of the righteous – a 'physical' body for an earthly kingdom and a 'spiritual' body for a heavenly kingdom.[69] In Isa. 26.19 and Dan. 12.2, resurrection is to an earthly kingdom and thus the resurrected are to have physical bodies. A similar thought is expressed in the Sibylline Oracles 4.181-82, where we read that the resurrection body is identical with the physical body: 'God himself shall fashion again the bones and ashes of men and shall raise up mortals once more as they were before.'

Other apocalyptists represent humanity's future life not in earthly but in supermundane terms. In these cases, as we have noted, the resurrection body is variously described as 'garments of glory' and 'life,' 'resplendent' and dwelling in 'shining light'. Such a change is envisioned 'either because a (person) goes direct to heaven at death or because the earthly kingdom in which he shares is only temporary and gives way to the age to come'.[70]

Outpouring of the Spirit

The bestowal of the Spirit in the messianic age was an apocalyptic hope. Ezekiel promises that God will pour out his Spirit on the house of Israel (36.26-27; 39.29) and resurrect the nation when he puts his Spirit within them to give them life (37.14). By putting within them his Spirit, they are to receive a new heart and be enabled to walk in obedience to God (36.27). In moral uprightness among God's people

---

[66] The wicked are 'to waste away' (51.5).

[67] As well as the counterpart 2 Enoch 22.8-10 teaches that the 'spiritual' body may co-exist with the 'physical' body. Enoch tells of his trip to the tenth heaven. He stands before God and hears the Lord command Michael to 'take Enoch from his earthily garments … and put him into the garments of my glory'. When this was done, Enoch reports, 'I looked at myself, and was like one of the glorious ones.'

[68] Russell, *The Method and Message of Jewish Apocalyptic*, p. 377.

[69] Russell, *The Method and Message of Jewish Apocalyptic* p. 376.

[70] Russell, *The Method and Message of Jewish Apocalyptic* p. 377.

the author of the Testament of Levi envisions that the spirit of holiness will be on the saints (18.11).

A similar promise is reiterated in Joel 2.28-32. The prophet may see this as a universal effusion of the Spirit. There is no apparent limitation to Jews only. It is to be on 'all flesh'.[71] The writer of the Testament of Benjamin also shares the same conviction. There is to be a universal gathering in the last temple. When God offers his salvation through 'the visitation of an only-begotten prophet, the Spirit of God shall pass on to the gentiles as fire poured forth' (9.2-4). Apparently 'only begotten prophet' refers to the Messiah. Thus, he is expected to be the bearer of the Spirit (cf. 1 Enoch 49.3; 62.2).

The Qumran community assigns the Spirit a prominent role in messianic times. The 'Spirit of truth' is to enlighten the heart of humans (1QS 3). God will pour upon people the 'Spirit of truth' and cleanse them from all abomination and falsehood (1QS 4). The hymnist maintained that he already possessed the gift of knowledge because of the Spirit that God has put in him (1QH 12). God also purifies him from sin: He cleansed his servant with the Holy Spirit and caused him to observe the commandments (1QH 16). An aspiration of the hymnist was to 'seek (Thy) spirit (of knowledge); cleaving to Thy Spirit of (holiness)' and 'hold fast to the truth of Thy Covenant' (1QH 16; lQS 4).

A passage about the star of Jacob in the Testament of Judah speaks also of the eschatological work of the Spirit: 'And the heavens shall be opened unto him, to pour out the spirit ... and ye shall be unto him sons in truth, and ye shall walk in his commandment first and last' (24.2-3).

A manifestation of the Spirit is expected in the messianic age. The Messiah is to be the bearer of the Spirit which he is to bestow on

---

[71] The phrase 'all flesh' could mean a universal outpouring of the Spirit since elsewhere the phrase in the Old Testament almost always includes all humanity (Gen. 6.12, 13; Deut. 5.26; Job 12.10; 34.14, 15; Ps. 65.2; Isa. 40.5, 6; Jer. 25.31; Ezek. 20.48; Zech. 2.13). This could be supported with Joel 2.32: 'All who call on the name of the lord shall be delivered.' However, 'all flesh' may be understood to be restricted by what follows – 'your' sons, 'your' daughters, etc. The outpouring is without distinction as to sex, age, or social class. Too, Peter, in his sermon, regarded the experience of the disciples as a fulfillment of Joel 2.8-32a and declared that this experience was available to all humanity (Acts 2.39).

humans.[72] The Spirit is to reveal the truth and transform humans to the very depths of their being so they will be led into righteousness.

The Final Judgment

The judgment is one of the major themes in apocalyptic literature. 'It is the great event towards which the whole universe is moving and which will vindicate once and for all God's righteous purpose for men and all creation.'[73] While there is no unanimity on details, generally it is expected that the everlasting kingdom of righteousness is to be established by God's intervention (Daniel 2-7; Isa. 24.27; Joel 3; Ps. Sol. 2.30-31; 15.12-13; 2 Baruch 85.12-13) and it is forensic as well as catastrophic.[74]

Such a denouement is forecast in 4 Ezra 7.113: 'But the Day of Judgment shall be the end of this age and the beginning of the eternal age that is to come.' Preceding the negation of the present world order Ezra expects a temporary messianic kingdom which is to last four hundred years and end with the death of the Messiah and all in whom there is human breath. Immediately the world will be turned into primeval silence seven days, and the new age will emerge (7.28-30; cf. 12.34). Then coinciding with the resurrection of those who sleep, the last judgment is expected to occur. 'The Most High shall be revealed upon the throne of judgment: (and then cometh the End) and compassion shall pass away …' (7.33).[75]

It is noteworthy that sometimes this judgment is universal, apparently including both Jews and non-Jews. 1 Enoch announces the punishment of every 'degenerated' world and the judgment and destruction on all who inhabit the earth (66.1-2). This goes beyond national and individual concerns, but in apocalyptic thought the nation and individual are judged by God. First Enoch 91.12, 13 is very

---

[72] Psalms of Solomon 17.42 anticipates that the Messiah is to be permanently endowed with the Spirit: 'For God will make him mighty by the means of (His) holy spirit' (cf. 1 Enoch 49.3; Test. of Jud. 24.2).

[73] Russell, *The Method and Message of Jewish Apocalyptic*, p. 380.

[74] Russell, *The Method and Message of Jewish Apocalyptic*, p. 380, observes that sometimes the forensic and catastrophic elements are distinguished and at other times they are confused.

[75] The author of Jubilees envisioned that the messianic kingdom will gradually be established as an earthly paradise, but he also expected it to end with God's judgment (23.30). However, 23.11 may suggest that the messianic kingdom is to follow the judgment. 1 Enoch 90.20-44 clearly indicates that the messianic reign on the earth is only established after the final judgment. Furthermore, 1 Enoch 43.3; 69.27-29 portray the Messiah as Judge.

nationalistic in outlook: judgment is executed on the oppressors of Israel and the Temple is to be restored. Following this, 'judgment shall be revealed to the whole world' (91.14a). The world is to be destroyed (91.14c), angels judged (91.15), and a new heaven appear (91.16) so that there will be no end to the new order (91.17). Thus, Enoch places side by side nationalistic and cosmic concerns.[76]

The final judgment may be described in national or universal terms, but individual judgment also has its place in apocalyptic thought. This individual interest, for example, is emphasized in 4 Ezra. According to 3.20-28, 'the evil heart' has caused the inhabitants of the city (Jerusalem) and 'all of his (Adam's) generations' to sin. Also, 3.38 refers to the sins of individual Israelites: 'We are all full of ungodliness', as well as a universal judgment. Ezra envisions the restoration of Israel. An angel explains to him, 'This woman, whom thou sawest, is Sion, whom thou now beholdest as a builded city' (10.44). However, included in Ezra's description of the Great Assize are references to 'faithfulness', 'deeds of righteousness' and 'deeds of iniquity' (4.34-35), which indicate individual judgment. 2 Enoch speaks of judgment of each person in precise terms: 'When all creation, visible and invisible, as the Lord created it, shall end, then every man goes to the great judgment' (65.6). On that occasion the actions and deeds of all people are weighed and measured (44.5). Every person will be judged for what they have done or left undone (1 Enoch 41.1-2). The righteous are promised eternal life in heaven and the wicked eternal torment in sheol (1 Enoch 99.11; 103.3-7; 104.2-3).

In the last judgment fallen angels and supernatural forces are judged. Demons and the Watchers are punished in that judgment (1 Enoch 16.1-2; cf. Jub. 5.10-11). The fallen angels are to be led off to the abyss of fire (1 Enoch 10.13) and they are to be cast into the abyss that is full of fire (1 Enoch 90.24).

Common to apocalyptic thought is that the establishment of God's kingdom involves war against the forces of evil. Sometimes these enemies are nothing more than human leaders and the nations under their direction (4 Ezra 12.33; 13.5-6; 2 Baruch 39.5-6; Ps. Sol. 17.21-22). Frequently, however, supernatural as well as human forces

---

[76] Enoch does not fully develop the two stages of the end time as the authors of 4 Ezra and 2 Baruch. For example, 2 Baruch suggests that the hope of national restoration by the Messiah is not the final stage of God's plan of salvation (40.3-4).

are meant (Jub. 23.29-30; 1 Enoch 91.12-13). The people at Qumran envisioned the final war as battle with supernatural powers. In the War Rule the nations with whom the community fights are described as 'the host of Belial'. By the aid of God and his angels they are finally defeated (1QM 1). The Rule of the community forecasts destruction of 'the Spirits of perversity' in the final judgment (1QS 3-4).

Thus, the impending day of visitation, when the wicked are judged and the opponents of Gad will be destroyed, looms large in apocalyptic theology. On that day, the apocalyptists expected that God's rule would be firmly established.

Conclusion

The survey reveals that apocalyptic is not a unified phenomenon. Though the apocalyptists differ in detail, a number of motifs are characteristic of their writings, such as the expectation that God's purpose is to be worked out within the historical process. This was the basis for their belief that all history – past, present, and future – was bound together and that God had preordained the entire course of events in history. Taking a deeply pessimistic view of history, they maintain that the present world is controlled by the powers of evil and is doomed to be destroyed. Consequently, apocalyptic theology makes a clear-cut differentiation between the present age and the coming age and between evil and good. Since it is always in the framework of monotheism, it is a limited dualism.

Prominence is given to the hope of the new age which is to be entirely different from the one that has gone before. A number of apocalyptists expect the messianic kingdom to be a kingdom on the earth and a temporary affair, spanning the time between the end of this world's kingdoms and the establishment of God's final order. Some look for God to come to the earth. Others expect the Messiah who is to destroy the evil power of Belial. The dawn of the messianic age is to be heralded by the woes of the Messiah – wars, earthquakes, religious apostasy, and many other disasters.

The messianic kingdom is a pre-ignition that moves in the direction of a total transformation of the spiritual condition and of the cosmos. Eschatological transformation normally envisions the resurrection of the individual and the bestowal of the Spirit that renews humans in the depth of their being. A number of apocalyptists see eschatological transformation as a return to primeval conditions that parallel either the period from creation (the beginning of humankind) to the sin of Adam or the period from the call of Abraham (the beginning of God's people) to Moses's time. God's purpose is expected to be worked out fully in the next world. The apocalyptists differ widely as to how the end is to be brought about, but absolutely fundamental to their thought is the conviction that God will ultimately prevail. Judgment is certain. Evil people will suffer eternal ruin for their evil deeds and the righteous will triumph and enjoy God's blessings with nothing to hinder their enjoyment.

4

THE APOCALYPTIC SCHEME OF THE TWO-AEONS IN 1 CORINTHIANS

This chapter is divided into six parts: (1) marks of the coming aeon, (2) Christ and the powers of 'this aeon', (3) the Spirit and the dawn of the coming aeon, (4) Christian existence at the turn of the ages, (5) the *Urzeit-Endzeit* scheme, and lastly (6) the expectation of the eschatological triumph of God. Before turning to the biblical texts, it is necessary to consider briefly two questions: (1) Paul's purpose in writing 1 Corinthians; and (2) the fact that he refers explicitly only to 'this age' (ὁ αἰών οὗτος) in 1 Corinthians and never to 'the coming ages' (ὁ μέλλων αἰών).

What was the basic problem at Corinth that prompted Paul to, write? John Hurd's reply is that it was the conviction that Christians would live until the return of Christ. He explains that Paul in his early preaching

> assured the Corinthians of the imminence of the *parousia*, but had said nothing of any need for a change of bodies or the resurrection to enter the Kingdom. There was no reason to talk of resurrection, since the time before the end was so short that there was no expectation of death; nor was there any reason to discuss a change of bodies, since this subject (as 1 Thessalonians and 1 Corinthians indicate) was dependent upon Paul's later explanation of the resurrection of those believers who had died.[1]

---

[1] Hurd, *The Origin of 1 Corinthians*, p. 285.

However, what evoked 1 Corinthians can be only an 'educated guess'. Since our understanding of why Paul wrote the letter will influence our interpretation of the passages, it is important that we state our point of view. The assumption here is that the letter arose out of problems created by Hellenistic enthusiasm that thought that eschatological conditions had already been fulfilled. Gunther Bornkamm observes that 'this movement at Corinth was anything but marginal and insignificant'.[2] He describes the mark of Corinthian enthusiasm as disavowal of responsible obligation toward the Christian community. Thus, it was an attempt to transcend the limits of time and history.[3] Eduard Schweizer, likewise, believes that enthusiasm was responsible for the trouble in the church at Corinth. 'Paul fights against the Corinthian enthusiasm which leaves space and time behind it.'[4]

According to the understanding of enthusiasts, what the apocalyptists expected from a future *parousia* has already been given in Christian baptism. Ernst Käsemann who, too, thinks that it was a kind of realized eschatology that evoked 1 Corinthians, corroborates this:

> It can of course today be taken as an established fact that the dominant group in Corinth imagined the goal of redemption to have been already attained with baptism, and that in its eyes the only further significance of Christian existence on earth was to provide a temporal resurrection of heavenly being … As participators in the resurrection and enthronement of Christ, they have been liberated from the old eon of death and its powers and translated into the new eon of the kingdom of Christ.[5]

What gave rise to 'present eschatology' at Corinth? It seems reasonable to assume that Paul's treaching at Corinth was cast in apocalyptic terms similar to those found in his letters. Traditional Jewish

---

[2] Bornkamm, *Paul*, p. 71. It is difficult to determine to what extent this enthusiasm was shared by the entire church. A number of scholars see in Paul's letters to the Corinthians evidence of mature Gnosticism in the second century sense. See the excursus, 'On the Problem of Gnosticism'.

[3] Bornkamm, *Paul*, p. 73.

[4] Eduard Schweizer, 'Dying and Rising with Christ', in Richard Batey (ed.), *New Testament Issues* (New York: Harper and Row, 1970), p. 180. See also in the same publication Hans Conzelmann, 'Current Problems in Pauline Research', pp. 143-44.

[5] Käsemann, 'On the Topic of Primitive Christian Apocalyptic', p. 119.

eschatology made a sharp temporal distinction between 'this age' and the future age. Even if Paul modified the apocalyptic scheme so that the coming age penetrates 'this age' his *kerygma* implied a strictly eschatological orientation for understanding Christian existence in this world. His preaching could have given rise to misconception by a Hellenistic audience at Corinth.[6] Schweizer observes that the Hebraic idea that history moves toward a goal was alien to those influenced by Greek thought and that, though the Corinthians may be described as dualists in terms of their belief in the existence of opposing heavenly and earthly spheres (but not detached aeons), they would have had trouble with the eschatological expectation that 'this age' will be superseded by another.[7] For them the receiving of the Spirit was more than a pledge of what is to come. It was a guarantee of the reality of the eschatological event. In Hellenistic thought the πνεῦμα was part of the heavenly world. Thus, according to Schweizer

> the coming of the Spirit is for him (the Hellenist) the breaking in of heavenly substance. If Jesus was the bringer of the Spirit, then He was the bearer of heavenly substance with which He endowed believers and united them with the heavenly world. A radical solution thus became possible for the first time. The point of the mission of Jesus was to bring the heavenly substance πνεῦμα into the world and attachment to Jesus is attachment to this substance of power, to the heavenly world. It is thus salvation.[8]

The specific problems to which Paul addresses himself in 1 Corinthians were only symptomatic of the fundamental error that apocalyptic hope was already realized and that the redeemed already transcended the world. Complete redemption has been conferred through sacramental baptism, and endowment with the πνεῦμα exempted them from the laws of life. They were representative of heavenly freedom in the world and gave no place for the traditional hope of the resurrection. Persons claiming to be full and reign as kings (4.8)

---

[6] M.H. Scharlemann, *Qumran and Corinth* (New York: Bookman Associates, 1962), p. 45, thinks that it was Apollos who introduced over-realized eschatology to the Corinthians.

[7] Eduard Schweizer, 'πνεῦμα', in Gerhard Kittel (ed.), *Theological Dictionary of the New Testament* (trans. and ed. Geoffrey W. Bromiley; Grand Rapids: Eerdmans, 1968), VI, p. 416. In subsequent footnotes this source will be referred to as *TDNT*.

[8] Schweizer, 'πνεῦμα', *TDNT*, p. 416.

believed that they had obtained 'fulfillment' that had placed them beyond judgment. The extreme individualism (10.14-15), the opposition to the conservative sexual ethic (6.12-13),[9] absence of consideration for the poor brothers at the Lord's Supper (11.17-18), and the overrating of *glossolalia* (Chaps. 12-14) and of sexual asceticism (7.1-7) testify to the belief that they had been liberated from all earthly ties and limitations. These were regarded as evidences of angelic status.[10] Paul's concern was to refute their error.

Furthermore, our insistence that Paul's belief in the apocalyptic doctrine of the two ages conditioned the entire perspective of 1 Corinthians gives rise to a terminological problem. If Paul was familiar with and accepted the doctrine of the ages, why does the phrase 'age to come' not occur in 1 Corinthians? The fact that Paul speaks of 'this age' (1 Cor. 1.20; 2.6; 3.18; 2 Cor. 4.4; Rom. 12.12), 'this world' (1 Cor. 3.19), and 'the present evil age' (Gal. 1.4) makes it probable that he knew the terminology of the two-age motif.[11] In Jewish thought 'the age to come' lies in the future and ushers in full and complete salvation. Paul does not apply it to the future as did the apocalyptists. For him 'the age' to come is not wholly future. To employ the term 'the coming aeon' would seem to obscure the ways the future age penetrates the present.

The teaching that 'the age to come' had been inaugurated and that its consummation was in the future would have been incomprehensible to the Greeks.[12] According to Paul's contemporaries a partial dawning of the new age was inconceivable. So, Paul found 'the age to come' to be an inappropriate description of either the present or the future and to avoid giving rise to confusion he makes no specific

---

9. Cf. Conzelmann, 'Current Problems in Pauline Research', in Richard Batey (ed.), *New Testament Issues* (New York: Harper and Row, 1970), p. 144, notes that this application of freedom is determined by the worldview behind it. 'One can manifest disdain of the gods by participating in their cults without any reverence for them in doing so; sexual freedom is a way to demonstrate that one has already soared above and beyond world and flesh.'

10. Cf. Käsemann 'On the Topic of Primitive Christian Apocalyptic', p. 120.

11. See Hermann Sasse, 'αἰών', *TDNT*, I, p. 203.

12. In Greek thought αἰών meant 'remote' or 'extended' or 'uninterrupted time'. 'αἰών', *TDNT*, I, p. 198. This term originally stood for a very long period of time; then it was employed to distinguish this world and the next. See Walter Bauer, William F. Arndt and Wilbur Gingrich, *A Greek-English Lexicon of the New Testament and Other Early Chrisitan Literature* (Chicago: University of Chicago Press, 1961), pp. 26-27. This title will be referred to subsequently as *BAG*.

reference to the future in aeon terminology. He variously names the old age 'this age', 'wisdom of the world', 'the wisdom of men', and 'the spirit of the world'.

Despite the fact that the term 'the coming age' never occurs in 1 Corinthians there is evidence of a terminological shift to other expressions, such as 'the power of God', 'the wisdom of God', 'the Spirit and power', and 'the Kingdom of God'. Something as sublime as the new age cannot be described except in terms of its qualities customarily as an antithesis to the characteristics of 'this age'.[13] Paul does not seem to develop a vocabulary for the new age that stands over against the moral and spiritual conditions of the old age except by indirect implication.

Marks of the Coming Aeon

Messianic Woes

It is well known that Paul understands that in his day Christ had begun to conquer the cosmic powers (1 Cor. 2.6), but the conquest is not yet complete (15.23-27). The Apostle exists in a time characterized by both suffering (1 Cor. 4.9-13; 2 Cor. 4.8-10; 6.8-10) and the enjoyment of the 'first fruits' of salvation (1 Cor. 2.18; 2 Cor. 6.2-3). He finds his situation to be characterized by tension between that which he has already experienced and that which is still outstanding. Thus, he believes that the death and resurrection of Jesus has inaugurated the ultimate event (1 Cor. 15.3, 20-21) and the torments and tribulations that Jewish apocalyptists expected to presage the 'end' are coming to pass in his own personal afflictions and agonies and in those of the Christian community.[14]

---

[13] See especially chapters 1-4 of 1 Corinthians where the antithesis is made explicit by Paul.

[14] This raises the question of how the sufferings of Paul are related to that of all believers. It may be argued there are no significant differences, but there may be basis for thinking that apostolic suffering and suffering of all believers are in some sense distinct. The distinctiveness of apostolic suffering would be derived from the distinctiveness of the apostolic office. Even so the suffering of Paul and the suffering of all believers stand together in a broad context. William A. Beardslee, *Human Achievement and Divine Vocation in The Message of Paul* (Naperville, IL: Alec R. Allenson, 1960), p. 114, corroborates this: 'While suffering is a mark of the apostle, in whom the tension between this age and the age to come shows itself at its sharpest, Paul regards his suffering as a calling or gift which he shares with all the church'.

The apocalyptic expectation of woes finds its expression in Paul in the believer's present experience of suffering with Christ.[15] 'The final curse had fallen on the Righteous One, and behind him it is not the unbelievers but believers who will henceforth be most directly assailed'.[16] Paul reminds his readers, 'I die every day! What do I gain if, humanly speaking, I fought with beasts at Ephesus?' (1 Cor. 15.31-32).[17] Here and in 4.9-13, the reference is to dangers and hardships that he has experienced in his apostolic work.[18] Introduced in both passages is the picture of the gladiatorial arena. In the first passage, this image is that of 'the savageness and ferocity of beasts' and makes 'vivid the nature of the human animosity and opposition that had confronted him at Ephesus'.[19] In the latter passage, the apostles are depicted as prisoners who have been 'sentenced to death' and who have become a 'spectacle'. They are represented as set forth 'last' to death, which does not mean that the apostles are the most insignificant of men. The term 'last' is associated with eschatological times (cf. 15.26; 45, 52); it relates to their place in the impending woes. This along with Paul's 'catalogue of difficulties' (4.10-13) serves to contrast the deprivations of the apostles with the enthusiasts at Corinth, who behaved as kings, assuming that the *eschaton* has already come and sin, suffering, and death are over (4.8).[20] While the Corinthians

---

[15] Without entering the debate about how Paul understands his suffering in relation to Christ's suffering let it suffice to state that the Apostle teaches that there is a substantial link between the sufferings of Christ and his own apostolic sufferings (2 Cor. 1.5; 4.10; Gal. 6.17). For a discussion on this question, see E. Güttgemanns, *Der leidende Apostel und sein Herr* (Göttingen: Vandenhoeck & Ruprecht, 1966), pp. 13-31.

[16] Michael Bouttier, *Christianity according to Paul* (Naperville, IL: Alec R. Allenson, 1966), p. 75.

[17] 1 Corinthians 15.30 refers to the physical hardships of the apostle. The phrase κατὰ ἄνθρωπον rendered 'humanly speaking' (15.32) probably indicates metaphorical usage. If his struggles with beasts at Ephesus is understood metaphorically, it refers to the gravity of the hazards endured. Cf. 2 Cor. 1.9, ἐν ἑαυτοῖς τὸ ἀπόκριμα τοῦ θανάτου ἐσχήκαμεν where the force of the perfect may indicate that the once-for-all sentence is a present and abiding reality. Cf. also 2 Cor. 4.10 πάντοτε τὴν νέκρωσιν τοῦ Ἰησοῦ ἐν τῷ σώματι περιφέροντες.

[18] The παθήματα χριστοῦ is by no means limited to the apostles (cf. 2 Cor. 1.5-7).

[19] Herbert M. Gale, *The Use of Analogy in the Letters of Paul* (Philadelphia: The Westminster Press, 1964), p. 95.

[20] The key word of 4.8 is 'already' (ἤδη) which occurs twice. The aorist tenses (ἐπλουτήσατε, ἐβασιλεύσατε) suggest eschatological fulfillment. The thought and

fancy themselves enthroned in the Kingdom of God, the apostles are engaged in the apostolic mission and are still laboring to enter the Kingdom of God. No relief is expected – 'To the present hour (ἄχρι τῆς ἄρτι ὥρας) we hunger and thirst, etc.' (4.11). 'I do not run aimlessly', Paul says elsewhere, 'I discipline my body and subdue it, lest after preaching to others I myself should be disqualified' (1 Cor. 9.26f).[21] The Apostles' present experience of suffering is a corrective to enthusiastic eschatology such as at Corinth and suggests in measure a realization of the messianic woes that are expected to precede the end.[22]

The 'birth pangs' associated with the messianic age are now imminent. Assuming this, Paul warns his readers in apocalyptic fashion that they must not get absorbed in the world. In its particular manner of manifestation, the world is already passing away (7.31). The time is short (7.29).[23] Because of the impending distress (τὴν ἐνεστῶσαν ἀνάγκην) he advises the Corinthians to remain in their present state whether this is circumcision or uncircumcision, freedom or slavery, marriage or singleness (7.17-28). This 'impending distress' must be eschatological woes that are present or that are just around the corner.[24] It seems that Paul is thinking of the imminent appearing (1 Thess. 5.2) and the preceding events – apostasy, wars, earthquake,

---

the language are eschatological. See C.K. Barrettt, *The First Epistle to the Corinthians*, p. 109.

[21] For Paul, suffering and hazards are fundamental to the preaching of the cross. Bouttier, *Christianity according to Paul*, p. 76, affirms this: '*Evangelion* and *thlipsis* go forward together; they are involved in each other, and can no more be separated in the epistles than can the Lord's cross and resurrection.'

[22] Käsemann, 'Beginnings of Christian Theology', p. 45, rightly insists that 'we have to distinguish the Corinthian illusionism very clearly from the apocalyptic rigorism which knows no salvation without earthly testing, allows it only to the sorely tried on earth'.

[23] ὁ καιρὸς συνεσταλμένος ἐστίν could mean a shortening of time, but the context does to suggest that Paul believed that God had shortened the time so that the righteous might remain faithful to the end. It apparently means that there is little time left. Each day the *parousia* draws closer. See Barrett, *The First Epistle ot the Corinthians*, p. 17.

[24] Barrett, *The First Epistle ot the Corinthians*, p. 175. In 1 Cor. 15.2 Paul exhorts the Corinthian believers to 'hold fast'. This could be an echo of apocalyptic admonitions to the faithful to endure steadfastly in face of external opposition and persecution. If the reference is not end-time woes, that there was some sort of pressure and uncertainty is borne out further by v. 58, 'be steadfast, immovable, always abounding in the work of the Lord'. They had not left behind 'this age' with its adversities.

pestilence, etc. – which usher it in (2 Thess. 2.8 cf., Mt. 24.4-15, 36-42).

With the messianic woes upon his readers, entanglement in earthly relations will have the effect of adding to the distress. 'From now on' their relation to all worldly engagements is the 'as if not' (7.29-31).[25] The old age is passing away. They do not belong to it and are to make ready for the *parousia* (1.8; 15.58). Paul's expectation parallels those apocalyptic writers who assumed that the coming of the Messiah will initiate a cosmic war at the end of time. Evil will be put down and the righteous vindicated, but in the remaining time before the *parousia* they might be aware of distress that they are to face. Eschatological perfection had not been attained as the enthusiasts thought and the old age will not pass out of existence until a period of severe eschatological upheaval has occurred. From the present time to the *parousia* no believer is exempted from the dangers of suffering, temptations and apostasy.[26]

The Resurrection of Christ

The *locus classicus* on the resurrection of the dead is 1 Corinthians 15.[27] An essential article of the Gospel is the resurrection of Christ (15.1-11). For Paul the death and resurrection of Christ are inseparable.

---

[25] Wolfgang Schrage, 'Die Stellung zur Welt bei Paulus, Epiktet und in der Apokalyptik: ein Beitrag zu I Kor. 7:29-31', *Zeitschrift für Theologie und Kirche* 61 (1964), pp. 125-54. Schrage argues that 1 Cor 7.29-31 is parallel to 4 Ezra 16.42-25 with respect to the motif of 'as if not'. It is generally agreed that the written form of 4 Ezra is no earlier than second century CE) but Schrage mantains that 4 Ezra is dependent on pre-Pauline apocalyptic tradition.

[26] As in Jewish apocalypticism Paul believes there must be a given amount of suffering fulfilled before the end can come. In 11.19 Paul states, 'for there must be (δεῖ) factions (αἱρέσεις) among you in order that those who are genuine among you may be recognized'. The context of this is the disputes over the Lord's Supper, Johannes Munck, *Paul and the Salvation of Mankind* (trans. Frank Clark; Richmond: John Knox Press, 1959), pp. 136-37, understands that δεῖ describes a divine, eschatological necessity and that Paul recognized that the disputes here were the first signs of the coming tribulations. Many in the church will fall away (cf. Mt. 24.10-11; Acts 20.30). For a discussion of the word δεῖ as a reference to eschatological necessities see Walter Grundmann, 'δεῖ', *TDNT*, II, pp. 22-23.

[27] H.W. Boers, 'Apocalyptic Eschatology in 1 Corinthians 15: an Essay in Contemporary Interpretation', *Interpretation* 21 (1967), p. 53, over-states the importance of this chapter for an adequate understanding of apocalyptic thought in the New Testament. 'In a sense, 1 Corinthians 15 can be regarded as a kind of test for apocalypticism in the New Testament. If it can be shown that apocalypticism is not determinative in the chapter, the case for nonapocalyptic eschatology would be made.

When he speaks primarily of the resurrection, the cross is in the back of his mind (15.3-5). Likewise, the resurrection is included in his discussion of the cross (1.22-23).[28] Jesus' resurrection is the 'first fruits' of the resurrection at the end of the age (15.29). Since first fruits indicates not only a pledge but also the actual beginning of the harvest,[29] the resurrection of Jesus is inseparable from that of the believers. They both belong to the same eschatological drama.

While Paul understands that the resurrection of Jesus is a mark that the world to come is already breaking into the present and that believers participate now in the risen life of Christ, his theological perspective is fundamentally different from the enthusiasts. Contrary to their belief, Paul maintains that the age to come remains an object of hope. Christian existence is characterized by the 'not yet' as well as the 'already'. Believers have been raised with Christ, but their mortal bodies have not been transformed. The enthusiasts' stress on the 'already' made it necessary for the Apostle to take up in 1 Corinthians 15 one of the prominent motifs in apocalyptic literature, the resurrection of the dead.[30]

A new epoch began with the resurrection of Christ. Even now the believers are risen with Christ. But Paul takes care to build in a safeguard against enthusiasm by speaking of the believers' participation in resurrection not in the perfect but future tense. As 'God raised the Lord he will raise (ἐγερεῖ) us through his power' (6.14). The believers' hope of eternal life is still a hope, for 'in Christ all shall be made alive' (ζωοποιηθήσονται 15.22). 'If in this life only we have hope in Christ, we are of all men to be pitied' (v. 19). There is a hint here of the doctrine of the two-ages. 'This life' is implicitly contrasted with a future existence. A decided apocalyptic note is struck in Paul's usage of the term κοιμάω ('to sleep', 'to fall asleep') to

---

[28] See Bultmann, *Theology of the New Testament* I, p. 292-93 and Manfred Kwiran, *The Resurrection of the Dead* (Basel: Friedrich Reinhardt Kommissionsverlag, 1972), pp. 77, 363.

[29] *BAG*, p. 80, observes that 'first fruits' becomes almost πρῶτος and renders ἀπαρχή τῶν κεκοιμημένων as 'the first of those who have fallen asleep' (1 Cor. 15.20). Murdoch E. Dahl, *The Resurrection of the Body* (Naperville, IL: Alec R. Allenson, 1962), p. 106, suggests that ἀπαρχή is a harvest term and that the final judgment is depicted in just such terms in, for example, Joel 3.13 and Rev. 14.15.

[30] Barrett, *First Epistle to the Corinthinas*, p. 353, claims that the two periscopes (vv. 23-38, 50-57) could have been an apocalypse which Paul divided in two and edited.

designate those who died (vv. 6, 18, 20, 51). It was because 'the word suggested a future awakening that Christians adopted it'[31] thereby reinforcing the incompleteness of the present.

Though the Apostle takes exception to the view that the resurrection of humanity has already taken place, he partially agrees with his opponents that the Christian has *now* more than hope and that in some sense the present is salvific. Observe that vv. 12, 13, and 20 speak of Christ as raised from the dead (ἐγήγερται ἐκ νεκρῶν). The perfect passive here of ἐγείρω signifies a once-for-all act with an abiding effect. In Paul's view the resurrection of Christ is the source of supernatural life, but what had happened did not, as his opponents thought, exclude a future resurrection. If they were right that eschatological conditions already had been completely fulfilled, 'then those … who have fallen asleep in Christ have perished' (v. 18). The issue is brought sharply into focus in vv. 20, 21, 23:

> But in fact, Christ has been raised from 'the dead, the first fruits of those who have fallen asleep. For as by a man came death, by a man has come also the resurrection of the dead … But each in his own order: Christ the first fruits, then at his coming those who belong to Christ.

According to Paul, there is discontinuity as well as continuity between present salvation and the future life. The term 'order' (τάγμα) is 'a military metaphor for a stage in the eschatological plan'.[32] In the divine plan the present is not the time of perfection and the full enjoyment of salvation, as Paul's opponents argue; but it is the time of benefits accruing from it. His resurrection is only one in a series of events in God's plan for the salvation of the believers. The vision of Paul includes the following: (1) this age ('this life', v. 19); (2) Christ's resurrection (v. 20); (3) resurrection of those who belong to Christ (v. 23); (4) messianic age (vv. 25-28); and (5) age to come (vv. 24- 28).[33]

---

[31] Robertson and Plummer, *A Critical and Exegetical Commentary of the First Epistle of St. Paul to the Corinthians*, p. 337. In conjunction with κοιμάω, it should be noted that the verb ἐγείρω ('to awaken from sleep', 'to wake up') is employed throughout the chapter. Cf. Dan. 12.2, though καθεύδω is used and not κοιμάω; 2 Ezra 7.32; 2 Bar. 30.2; Isa. 26.19. The figure 'sleep' has previously been used in some contexts without any belief in the resurrection (Test. Joseph 20.4; Jub. 23.1).

[32] Dahl, *The Resurrection of the Body*, p. 126.

[33] In v. 25, Paul uses the word δεῖ (also v. 53) which, says Dahl, *The Resurrection of the Body*, p. 109, indicates 'the eschatological necessity for the fulfilment of God's

Paul's argument is that Jesus' deliverance from death is the first (ἀπαρχή) and that the bestowal of life (v. 22) is reserved until the *parousia* of Christ (v. 23). At the time of Christ's *parousia* Christians will be raised. Thereupon the end (τὸ τέλος) of 'this age' and the final Kingdom of God (v. 24) will ensue.[34] This had not been accomplished. Jesus has not subdued all cosmic powers (vv. 25-27). Death, the last enemy, maintains its power and has not been brought under the sovereignty of Christ.[35] Christ's reign in the present time is incomplete and the time of perfection is located by Paul at the *parousia*. Thus, the Apostle believes, as Barrett insists, that the situation in which he and fellow-Christians lived was too complicated to be reduced to a simple straight line or curve. 'It was and it was not, the age to come, since the resurrection had already happened (in the person of Jesus), yet had not happened (for the rest of mankind)'.[36]

The Eschatological Temple

Apocalyptic writers anticipated that in the last times God would build a new temple in which he would dwell (Ezek. 37.26-27; 1 Enoch 90.29; 91.13; Jub. 1.17, 29). Bultmann reminds us that the Christian community for Paul is an eschatological congregation. It is

---

purpose in creation and redemption.' Here again is the apocalyptic motif of determinism.

[34] With respect to the expression τὸ τέλος (v. 24), there have been a number of suggestions. Some would hold to a threefold resurrection of the dead – of Christ, of those who belong to him, and of 'the rest' – presumably the wicked dead. This raises the question of whether Paul in this chapter teaches a resurrection of the unrighteous dead. It is possible that the clause 'in Christ shall all be made alive' (v. 22) is meant to include the unbelievers. There is no uniformity in other apocalyptic literature on this matter. Some sources would hold only to the resurrection of the righteous (Isa. 26.19) while others teach the raising of two classes, 'some to everlasting life, and some to shame and everlasting contempt' (Dan. 12.2). This latter teaching is also found in 2 Baruch 51. Other explanations of the term τὸ τέλος need not be considered here except for the only live option to the preceding suggestion – namely, that this term is to be translated 'the end' and is to be understood as marking the time when 'this age' gives way to the 'age to come'. It would appear that this is more in line with the immediate context. Paul, it seems, is not too concerned with the resurrection of the wicked dead in this chapter. In point is 2 Bar. 30.1, which apparently is in line with this latter view: the righteous who have been resurrected 'know that the time has come of which it is said, that it is the consummation of the times'.

[35] Käsemann, 'On the Topic of Primitive Christian Apocalyptic', p. 132, argues that behind Paul's resurrection theology lies the apocalyptic concern as to whom the lordship of the world belongs.

[36] C.K. Barrett, *From The First Adam To Last* (New York: Charles Scribner's Sons, 1962), p. 4.

established by an eschatological, supermundane event, namely by the Christ-event and stands not in continuity with the old aeon but rather stands within the new aeon, for the Christ-event brings to an end the old age and inaugurates the eschatological.[37]

According to Bultmann, Paul views the church as the eschatological community. Through its response to the call of the gospel the church has been taken out of the fallen world and incorporated into Christ.[38] This understanding of the church is supported by Paul's application of the apocalyptic notion 'temple of God' to the community of believers (1 Cor. 3.16).[39] It is erected on the foundation of Christ (3.10-11) and thus is the eschatological community through its relationship with the Christ-event.

When Paul speaks of the church as the temple of God, he understands that it is a community that has experienced and acknowledges the power of God expected in the last days. Similar to apocalyptic hope, Paul believes that God dwells in a new temple, the community of believers. God's power has already broken into 'this age', and God's Spirit indwells the corporate fellowship. The Apostle insists that a mark of the eschatological congregation is the new quality of life produced by the presence of the Spirit. As he reminds the Corinthians, God's temple is holy, you are that temple, and you must be holy (3.16, 17). Under the illusion that the *eschaton* has arrived, the enthusiasts at Corinth disown all responsibility for the present life of the Christian community and stir up discord by the claim to true wisdom (1.20; 2.5, 6; 3.18). As a result, they are destroying the eschatological temple which Paul also describes as 'God's building' (θεοῦ οἰκοδομή, 3.9) in which the Spirit dwells (3.16). A central concern of Paul is, therefore, that all things be done toward the building up (οἰκοδομεῖν) of the church (4.5, 26). In apocalyptic fashion Paul

---

[37] Bultmann, *Theology of the New Testament*, I, pp. 308-11. Cf. Rudolph Bultmann, *Essays, Philosophical and Theological* (New York: Macmillian Company, 1955), pp. 199-200.

[38] Bultmann, *Essays, Philosphical and Theological*, pp. 204-205 and *Theology of the New Testament*, I, p. 308.

[39] Paul also uses the metaphor 'temple of God' with reference to the Christian community (6.19): In the same context Paul connects Christ with the image of God's temple. He insists that God's raising Christ from the dead requires that every Christian avoid immorality (6.13-14), and he alludes to the redemptive death of Christ by reminding the Corinthians that they have been 'bought with a price'. Their sexual union with prostitutes is tantamount to profaning the temple dedicated to God.

offers a corrective by warning the enthusiasts that they are not beyond judgment. Each is accountable to God for his actions. If anyone
destroys (φθείρει) the local congregation, God will destroy (φθείρει̂)
him (3.16). Judgment is reserved for the Lord, who in the day of
judgment will bring to light all that is hidden. 'Then every man will
receive his commendation from God' (4.3-5).

It is, therefore, Paul's conviction that the 'Christian fellowship' is
the eschatological temple. As such it is a mark of the dawn of the
coming age, but it is not understood as already complete. It exists as
an eschatological phenomenon created by the redeeming power of
God, but it awaits the consummation of God's act of redemption
which has been inaugurated but not yet concluded. Paul maintains
that judgment remains an eschatological fact (6.2, 3; 11.32) and reminds his opponents at Corinth that those who are guilty of destroying the church, God's temple, are to suffer dire consequences.

The Ultimate Sign: The Holy Spirit

The eschatological temple, the church, is the dwelling place of the
divine presence. When Paul became a Christian, he 'entered a new
community and in the pneumatic phenomena that marked the life of
that community, in its enthusiasm and power he saw proof of the
advent of the Age to Come. The active presence of the Spirit in
power was a mark of the *Endzeit*.'[40] Unlike much Jewish thought that
concentrated on the future in contrast to an empty present, Paul discerns that the future age has broken into the present in the action of
the Holy Spirit.[41] The idea of the Spirit unites both the present and
future since the Spirit is the power of the future in the present. This
seems to be the thrust of Bultmann's statement that the Spirit 'may
be called the power of futurity'.[42]

---

[40] Davies, *Paul and Rabbinic Judaism*, p. 126. Cf. also *Christian Origins and Judaism*, p. 174, where Davies contends that for Paul the Spirit is the sign of the End par excellence.

[41] N.Q. Hamilton, *The Holy Spirit and Eschatology in Paul* (Edinburgh: Oliver and Boyd, 1957), p. 23. Edward Schweizer, 'πνεῦμα', *TDNT*, VI, p. 422, stresses that in the primitive Christian community the Spirit was the sign of that which is yet to come. 'Since the event of the resurrection at the end of the ages is no longer an indefinite hope, the present reality of the Spirit is a pledge of the reality of what is to come.' See also his essay, 'Gegenwart des Geistes und eschatologische Hoffnung', *The Background of the New Testament and its Eschatology* (ed. W.D. Davies and David Daube; Cambridge: Cambridge University Press, 1964), pp. 505-506.

[42] Bultmann, *Theology of the New Testament*, I, p. 334.

For Paul the Spirit belongs primarily to the future, but the present activity of the Spirit means eschatological fulfillment and the present possibility of eschatological fulfillment and the present possibility of eschatological life.[43] Too, the Spirit, the power of the new aeon, is a sign that reaffirms the approaching end. As in apocalyptic thought, Paul often speaks of the Spirit in terms of power and associates pneumatic activity closely with the Messiah. This is evident in 1 Corinthians. The proclamation of the Gospel at Corinth was 'in demonstration of Spirit and power' (ἐν ἀποδείξει πνεύματος καὶ δυνάμεως, 2.4) so that their faith wrought by the Spirit might rest 'in the power (δυνάμει) of God' (2.5). The terms 'power' and 'Spirit' are essentially synonyms.[44] In light of this Paul teaches that the Spirit worked instrumentally in Jesus' resurrection. 'God raised the Lord ... by his power (δυνάμεως; 6.14; cf. Rom. 1.4).[45] Elsewhere he employs the term 'spiritual' (πνευματικόν) to describe the resurrection body of the believer (15.44-45). In Paul πνευματικόν always has reference to the activity of the Holy Spirit (1 Cor. 7.14; 12.1; 14.1; Rom. 1.11; Gal. 6.1; Col. 1.9). The πνεῦμα–δύναμις relationship in Paul's thought makes it clear why he claims that the 'spiritual body' is to be raised ἐν δυνάμει (15.43).

While noting the close connection of the Spirit's activity with Jesus' resurrection and that of the believers, we must not overlook the fact that Paul teaches that the present work of Christ is pneumatic: 'The last Adam became a life-giving Spirit' (πνεῦμα ζῳοποιοῦν; 15.45).[46] As the believers' pneumatic existence is to begin at their resurrection so Christ apparently became a life-giving Spirit at his resurrection. It is the Spirit that brings a new existence to humanity (5.5) Paul reminds the Corinthians 'that God's Spirit dwells in you' (3.16). Since there is a close link between the Spirit and Christ in Pauline

---

[43]Hamilton, *The Holy Spirit and Eschatology in Paul*, pp. 26-27.

[44] The terms are a hendiadys. Note that in 1 Thess. 1.5 they are in reverse order.

[45] The prepositional phrase, διὰ τῆς δυνάμεως αὐτου, should be construed with ἤγειρεν as well as ἐξεγερεῖ. See Robertson and Plummer, *A Critical and Exegetical Commentary on the First Epistle of St. Paul to the Corinthians*, p. 124.

[46] πνεῦμα ζῳοποιοῦν of 1 Cor. 15.45 must reflect the influence of the apocalyptic image of the eschaton when God's Spirit will impart life: 'And I will put my Spirit within you and you shall live' (Ezek. 27.14). Hamilton, *The Holy Spirit and Eschatology*, pp. 3-4, maintains that as Christ mediates the reality of God that the life-giving Spirit mediates the reality of Christ. Cf. Schweizer, 'πνεῦμα', *TDNT*, VI, pp. 433-34.

thought, the present possession of Spirit is interchangeable with 'Christ in you, the hope of glory' (Col. 1.27).[47]

Thus, Paul sees the eschatological power of God as already operative in 'this age'. Indeed, for him the Spirit is the chief mark that the new age is dawning. However, in his typical manner, he continues his polemic against enthusiasm. He contends that present fulfillment is not the future secured, but it provides a firm foundation for hope of eschatological fulfillment. The presence of the Spirit marks the end of the old aeon and the inauguration of the new. It marks the community of believers as belonging to the timespan between the resurrection of Jesus and the *parousia*, of which the Spirit is a token and pledge.[48]

Christ and the Powers of 'This Aeon'

The Cosmic Lordship of Christ
Paul operated with an apocalyptic-demonic understanding of the world order.[49] He believed that the present world order lay in the grips of 'evil cosmic forces which were bent on the destruction of mankind and of the world itself' (1 Cor. 2.6, 8).[50] Clearly, Paul was convinced that the death and resurrection of Christ constitute the overthrow of the demonic powers. Christ is described as 'destroying every rule and every authority and power' (15.24). This, of course, refers to the *parousia*, but the process has been inaugurated by the cross and resurrection. 'The rulers of this age'[51] are already passing

---

[47] The eschatological concept 'glory' is closely connected with the Spirit (1 Cor. 15.43-44; 2 Cor. 3.8, 17-18). It is an apocalyptic *terminus technicus*. See Gerhard Kittel, 'δόξα', *TDNT*, II, p. 247.

[48] See Schweizer, 'πνεῦμα', *TDNT*, VI, p. 422 and G.W. Lampe, *The Seal of the Spirit* (New York: Longmans, Green and Company, 1951), p. 46.

[49] Thackery, *The Relation of St. Paul to Contemporary Jewish Thought*, pp. 142-78. Paul's interest in angels and invisible powers shows his affinity with one prominent apocalyptic interest (1 Cor. 4.9; 6.2-3; 11.10; 13.1; Rom. 8.38; Gal. 3.19).

[50] Russell, *The Message and Method of Jewish Apocalyptic*, p. 267. In a typical apocalyptic vein Paul in 1 Cor. 10.19-21 refers to demons in connection with idolatry and in 7.5 calls attention to the work of Satan who may tempt married couples that abstain from conjugal relations. However, apocalyptic does not venture the thought of 5.5 where Paul teaches that the sentence imposed by Satan on the sinner is for the purpose of his salvation. See Werner Foerster, 'σατανάς', *TDNT*, VII, p. 162.

[51] Scholars have disagreed whether 'rulers of this age' should be understood as political rulers or spirit powers. The context favors the latter, but the study of the background of Paul's demonology will reveal that ἀρχαί, ἐξουσίαι, θρόνοι and similar designations of authority are relevant to the interpretation of οἱ ἄρχοντες in 1 Cor. 2.8. Oscar Cullmann, *The Early Church* (trans. A.J.B. Higgins and Stanley

awy (καταργουμένων, 2.6).[52] One effect of the breaking in of this apocalyptic reality is that judgment has already been passed and the cosmic powers themselves are being subjected. Paul's reliance on apocalyptic tradition makes it probable that 2.6 refers to a heavenly as well as earthly battle.[53] Christ's victory has cosmic significance. The old aeon with its powers has been rendered ineffective, and Christ is now Lord of the world. The confession, Jesus is Lord (12.3),[54] rests on the belief that he was exalted above all other gods and lords (8.5, 6).

Clearly, Paul is convinced that already Christ is enthroned, to exercise dominion in 'this age'. Yet with apocalyptic as the background he argues that Christ's lordship is decisive for the future. It is evident that though the evil powers have been dispossessed they have not been destroyed. Death continues to exist, but Christ must continue to reign (βασιλεύειν) until it is brought to naught as the last enemy (15.25-26).[55] 'All things are put in subjection under him' (15.27).[56] In light of the fact that victory is to be complete and universal, Käsemann contends that the eschatological end is still outstanding. He goes on to say: 'The term (*basilei Christi*) which Paul, obviously

---

Godman; Philadelphia: Westminster Press, 1966), p. 121, argues that in 1 Cor. 2.8, οἱ ἄρχοντες refers to both human rulers and spirit powers that lie behind them: 'They were already behind the state authorities who brought Christ to the cross. They are the ἄρχοντες τοῦ αἰῶνος τούτου, who crucified the "Lord of glory" in their ignorance of the "hidden wisdom of God" (1 Cor. 2.7, 8). Herod and Pilate were merely their executive organs.' This posits a limited dualism which conforms to Paul's thought.

[52] 1 Corinthians 15.24-25 also has in view cosmic warfare.

[53] The preeminence of the title κύριος was favored both by the antithetical analogy to the many 'lords' of the Roman world and by the use of it by Hellenistic Jews to render the tetragrammaton. Christ's lordship implies that Psalm 110 is not without significance.

[54] Cullmann, *The Early Church*, p. 122.

[55] Presumably Paul expects Christ to eliminate his other enemies before it is death's turn. The word 'last' (ἔσχατος, v. 26) is used anarthrously with 'enemy' (ἐχθρός) for, according to Robertson and Plummer, *A Critical and Exegetical Commentary on the First Epistle of St. Paul to the Corinthians*, p. 356, 'there can be only one last'.

[56] There is no hint in the passage that Christ's developing reign falls between the *parousia* and the final kingdom of God. Paul argues that his reign is consummated in the *parousia*.

borrowed from tradition, is apocalyptic, as is also the view which sees in the Kyrios not the cultic Lord but the exalted cosmocrator'.[57]

The Lordship of Christ in the Church

According to Paul, Christ is the Lord of the church. Christians are the ones who call on the name of the Lord (1.2; cf. Joel 2.32). The Spirit teaches them to say one thing: 'Jesus is Lord' (12.3). The designation of the Eucharist as κυριακὸν δεῖπνον implies the same – the authority of the Lord is set up over believers and acknowledged by them (11.20). Paul regards ministers of the gospel as servants of the Lord (3.5). In his own ministerial activity, the apostle is alert to the will of the Lord (4.19), and he believes that pleasing the Lord should be given first priority in the Christian life.[58]

Christ is now Lord in the church, and the church is his body (12.27). As his body the church is identified with Christ. In Christ the believers, the renewed humanity, have recovered their lost lordship. This is due to Christ's apocalyptic triumph through death and resurrection. His people are no longer enslaved by cosmic evil powers. Thus, Paul claims that everything belongs to the Christian community on earth and in heaven (3.23).

To what extent can this be claimed for the church? The believers are subject to the viscissitudes of this age – suffering, temptations, and death. Paul recognizes that death still holds the field (15.26). As Käsemann says, 'Within it (the church) all the powers except death … have forfeited their lordship to the Christ, while they still reign around it'.[59] On the basis of 1 Cor. 6.13, 'The body is for the Lord and the Lord for the body', he insists that according to Paul Christians have a role in subjecting the powers.

> In bodily obedience of Christians … in the life of everyday, it becomes visible that Christ is the Lord of the world … They

---

[57] Käsemann, 'On the Topic of Primitive Christian Apocalyptic', p. 129. Some have thought that Paul's *kyrios* Christology is derived from the imperial cultus. Reginald H. Fuller, *The Foundations of New Testament Christology* (New York: Charles Scribner's Sons, 1965), pp. 230-31, rejects this as the source. Messiahship and lordship are similar categories. The former is strictly Jewish, and the latter probably is too, especially since Paul understands Christ's lordship eschatologically (1 Cor. 1.8; 5.5). His predilection to use κύριος in 1 Corinthians could have been due to the presuppositions of his opponents.

[58] It is not always clear when Paul uses the title κύριος whether Christ or God is in view.

[59] Käsemann, 'On the Topic of Primitive Christian Apocalyptic', p. 130.

(Christians) testify to his lordship as that of the cosmocrator and thereby provide an anticipatory sign of the ultimate future of the reality of the resurrection and of the unrestricted *regnum Christi*.[60]

Contrary to the thought of radical enthusiasm, the old world remained. The powers had been dethroned but not wiped out. Any advance made by the church before the *parousia* may be countered by the evil powers. Paul recognizes that in *pre-parousia* times the church may find itself retreating. True to apocalyptic, he is not overly optimistic.

The Title 'Lord' and the *Parousia*

The title 'Lord' appears frequently in connection with the *parousia* (1 Cor. 1.8; 4.4, 5; 11.26, 32; Phil. 4.5; 1 Thess. 4.6; 15-16). Paul portrays the *parousia* as the day in which the Lord will judge and triumph over all adversaries (1 Cor. 1.8; 3.13; 15.23-24).[61]

Yet, as we have seen, the lordship of Christ is already operative. The decisive battle has been fought and won in his death and resurrection. Though Paul believes that Christ has subjugated the spirit-world and has begun to rule in the present age, the hostile forces are still active and will not be finally destroyed until the *parousia*.[62] So the apostle expects Christ to continue his redemptive activity until the last adversary has been destroyed (15.26). In his vision this goal is not accomplished until the *parousia*. The expectation of the *parousia* may be meaningless for enthusiasm but not for Paul. 'Paul,' declares Käsemann, 'cannot and will not speak of an end of history that has

---

[60] Käsemann, 'On the Topic of Primitive Christian Apocalyptic', pp. 131-32.

[61] The expression 'the second man is from heaven' (1 Cor. 15.47) ought to be understood in terms of the *parousia* rather than the incarnation. Cf. Robertson and Plummer, *A Critical and Exegetical Commentary on the First Epistle of St. Paul to the Corinthians,* p. 374. It is possible that the eucharistic invocation *Marantha* emphasizes both Christ's presence at the meal and at the *parousia*. See Reginald H. Fuller, *The Foundation of New Testament Chrsitology*, p. 157.

[62] Harry Argus Kennedy, *St. Paul's Conception of the Last Things* (London: Hodder and Stoughton, 1904), pp. 193-94, sees an intimate connection of the Apostle's idea of judgment with the prophetic conception of the 'Day of the Lord', but he notes two differences: 'Only on the one hand, the horizon has immensely widened. On the other hand, the somewhat vague pictures of God's judgement which the prophets clothe in various forms, have given place to the definite intervention of the exalted Lord, Jesus Christ armed with complete authority.' This suggests that apocalyptic is a factor in Paul's view of time and his story, but he does modify apocalyptic dualism in his conception of the Christ-event.

already taken place, but that (sic) he does regard the time of the end as having dawned'.[63]

The Spirit and the Dawn of 'the Coming Aeon'

The Spirit and the Awareness of 'the Coming Age'

For Paul the giving of the Spirit is closely linked to the Christ-event: the death and resurrection of Jesus Christ. Without the resurrection, the cross would have been a disaster (1 Cor. 15.4). The cross opened the way for the coming of the Spirit (Gal. 3.13, 14). Already we have observed in Pauline thought a very close connection between the Spirit and the resurrection.[64]

Paul describes what God did in Christ as a mystery of God (μυστήριον τοῦ θεοῦ 2.1).[65] Admittedly the meaning of the Christ-event lay hidden in God, but Paul insists that the Spirit revealed to him his message, the hidden things of God (2.10) and that only those who have the Spirit can understand what God did in Christ (2.11-12). The rulers of this age acted foolishly because they were ignorant of what God was doing in the cross (2.6, 7). The believers who have received the Spirit from God understand what is taught to them by the Spirit (2.12). The very manner in which Christian teaching is done is not by human wisdom but by the Spirit (2.13). By contrast unspiritual men are blind to the significance of what God did in Christ because they lack the Spirit.

The reason the rulers did not understand what they did was that they belonged to 'this age' (2.8). The Christians have the Spirit of God, not 'the spirit of the world' (2.12), that is, 'the wisdom of this age' (2.6). By the Spirit the early Christians were aware that the new age had dawned. But their present enlightenment by the Spirit caused them to look forward to the time when impartial knowledge gives away to a more perfect understanding (13.12).

---

[63] Käsemann, 'On the Topic of Primitive Christian Apocalyptic', p. 129.

[64] See 1 Cor. 6.14 where δύναμις is equivalent to πνεῦμα. Another synonym for πνεῦμα is δόξα (Rom. 6.4). Both passages teach that the Spirit was instrumental in the resurrection of Christ.

[65] The concept μυστήριον has been taken into the preaching of the primitive church from apocalyptic tradition and corresponds to the Hebrew רז (secret) which designates the eschatological mystery of God's decree (Dan. 2.18, 19, 27, 30, 47; 4.9). The mystery cults had no eschatological dimension, but apocalyptic mysteries have an eschatological cosmic orientation. See Günther Bornkamm, 'μυστήριον, μυέω', *TDNT,* IV, pp. 813-16.

The Spirit and the Consumation of 'this Aeon'

The focus here is on the connection of the Spirit with (1) the assurance of hope and (2) the kingdom. By the Spirit all believers have been baptized into the eschatological event of Christ's death and resurrection and have been given the Spirit (1 Cor. 12.13), a sign that they belong already to the new age. Fundamentally, this is Paul's position. However, to limit the claims of enthusiasm that all eschatological hope had been fulfilled, he emphasizes that the Spirit gives validity to and constitutes the believers' hope of glory (cf. 2 Cor. 1.22; 5.5). The Spirit is the substance of Christian hope – a hope that will be realized when the physical gives away to the spiritual (1 Cor. 15.44-45). In contrast to the first Adam, Christ is said to have become a life-giving Spirit by the resurrection. This assumes that those that belong to him will experience a similar transition from their earthly existence to their heavenly existence. Thereupon the believers are to receive a 'spiritual body' (σῶμα πνευματικόν) of which present work of the Spirit in the church is a pledge. The reason is that Paul sees Christ's resurrection as the 'first-fruits' (ἀπαρχή) of the resurrection of the believers and links both closely with the activity of the Spirit (6.14; 15.20-23). Thus, the Spirit is the Christian's assurance of the consummation of the age as well as the sign of the arrival of the new age.

Furthermore, this is seen in Paul's use of the apocalyptic idea of the kingdom of God. His exposition of it relates the Spirit to the consummation of this age. N.Q. Hamilton observes that in Pauline thought the Spirit takes the place of βασιλεία of the Gospels, for the Spirit of Christ is the inner dynamic which implements God's reign.[66] Paul sees the kingdom of God as a present reality. He explains that it does not operate by human eloquence but by the power (δύναμις) of the Spirit (4.20 cf. 2.4; Rom. 14.17). The church has already been drawn into its transcendent power by the Spirit. At the same time the Spirit is the pledge of the final rule of God which remains an object of hope for the church. Observe that Paul warns the Corinthians that the kingdom of God is something to inherit or fail to inherit (1 Cor. 6.9, 10). In this passage, the term 'inherit' (κληρονομεῖν) appears twice and both are in the future tense (cf. Gal. 5.21). It is in the sphere of God's reign that eschatological blessing is to be 'inherited'. God's

---

[66] Hamilton, *The Holy Spirit and Eschatology in Paul*, p. 38.

messianic rule began in the death and resurrection of Christ. Now Christ reigns (βασιλεύειν) as king and is to continue until all enemies are put under his feet (1 Cor. 15.25). The perfect rule of God is the goal of redemption, but through the Spirit believers already share in his kingdom (1 Cor. 4.20; Col. 1.13; Rom. 14.17).

Christian Existence at the Turn of the Age

Epistemological Dualism: Wisdom and Foolishness

To the Corinthians Paul writes that the 'ends of the ages' (τὰ τέλη τῶν αἰώνων)[67] had come upon them (1 Cor. 10.11). The old age and the new have touched each other; the end of the old (the plural indicates the termination of the epochs in it) coincides with the inception of the new.[68] So, the time between resurrection and the *parousia* is thought by Paul to be a time the two ages – this age and the age to come – overlap.[69] The cosmic apocalyptic event at the end of the ages had already intervened in Jesus Christ to bring the blessing of the new age in advance. Paul understands that the Corinthian believers, though still living in this age, belong to the new eschatological time. Since they exist in a time characterized by the mingling of the two ages, it is necessary to understand their existence as a dual one.

This is seen in Paul's epistemological concern (1 Cor. 1.17 – 4.20). The contrast between 'this age' and the 'age to come' is implicit when Paul speaks of the things present (ἐνεστῶσα) and of things future (μέλλοντα, 3.22). But the antithesis is made explicit by his emphasis on two ways of knowing. 'The wisdom of the world' (1.20; 3.18) 'the wisdom of men' (2.5; 1.19), 'a wisdom of this age' (2.6; 3.18),[70] and 'human wisdom' (3.13) are set over against 'the wisdom of God'

---

[67] The expression is equivalent to the Hebraic idea 'end of days' (cf. Dan. 12.13). See H.L Strack and Paul Billerbeck, *Kommentar zum Neuen Testament aus Talmud und Midrasch* IV (Müchen: C.H. Beck'sche Verlagsbuchhanlung, 1961), p. 416-17.

[68] Jean Héring, *The First Epistle of Saint Paul to the Corinthians* (trans. A.W. Heathcote and P.J. Allcock; London: The Epworth Press, 1962), p. 89.

[69] Schoeps, *Paul: The Theology of the Apostle in Light of Jewish Religions History*, p. 99, observes 'This mingling of the two ages constitiutes the distinctive eschatological standpoint of Pauline theology'.

[70] 'This age' (αἰών) may also bc described as 'this world' (κόσμος). In 1 Cor. 3.18, 19 the two are synonymous. Héring, *The First Epistle of Saint Paul to the Corinthians*, p. 10. However, in 2 Cor. 5.19, κόσμος signifies 'the world of men' since we are told 'God was in Christ reconciling the world to himself, not counting their sins against them'.

(1.21, 24), 'a secret and hidden wisdom of God' (2.7) and 'words …
taught by the Spirit' (2.13). No doubt, this contrast of the wisdom of
God with human wisdom is due to the prominence of the wisdom
theme among the Corinthians. In accord with their enthusiastic
claims they believed God had granted them all the blessings of the
new age including full and complete knowledge. Supposedly from a
superior position they looked down on the apostles (4.10). Paul sees
factions among them as evidence that they are not as wise and spiritual as they assume. They were quarreling (ἔριδες) over their teach-
ers saying, 'I belong to Paul' or 'I belong to Apollos' or 'I belong to
Cephas' or 'I belong to Christ'' (1.12). Thus, they 'boast of men' and
are 'puffed up in favor of one against another' (3.21; 4-5). Their
boasting in 'men', however, implies that they are boasting in their own
wisdom (3.18-19; 4.7-8).

Paul's first preaching of the word of the cross at Corinth provides
the framework in which the Apostle corrects those who proudly
claim access to a wisdom that secured a perfected salvation (τέλειοι,
2.6) and a level of spirituality (πνευματικοί, 3.1) that led to a haughty
indifference to the flesh which manifested itself in two extremes, either indulgence or asceticism (6.12; 7.1). God acted eschatologically
in his disclosure of His wisdom and power in the cross. Paul speaks
of the word of the cross as a μυστήριον. This message was concealed
from the world and its rulers but revealed to those endowed with the
Spirit of God (2.10-11). The radical antithesis of wisdom of 'this
age' to God's hitherto hidden wisdom was manifested by the inability
of the rulers of 'this age' to understand God's pre-temporal plan for
the salvation of the world. Consequently, they crucified the 'Lord of
glory' (2.8;[71] cf. Col. 1.15).

Moreover, the event of the crucifixion has a twofold effect,
namely, to those who are perishing (οἱ ἀπολλύμενοι) it is the power

---

[71] This expression 'Lord of glory' seems to have been borrowed from the apocalyptic thought of Enoch, in which this title is given to God (1 Enoch 22.14; 25.3,
7; 27.3, 4; 63.2; 75.3). C.T. Craig's observation in *First Epistle to the Corinthians* (Interpreter's Bible, Vol. 10; New York: Abingdon, 1954), p. 38, is worth quoting.
'Possibly Paul shared ideas similar to those in the Ascension of Isaiah 10.11, where
the heavenly Christ is not recognized by the powers as he descends through the
heavens. Not understanding God's mystery, these principalities and powers had
conspired to bring Jesus to his death … These rulers are to be identified with "the
elemental spirits" of the universe (Gal. 4.3, 9; Col. 2.8).'

of God (1 Cor. 1.18, 2 Cor. 2.15-16).[72] It is true that 'the Christian
has experienced the supernatural power released by the cross'.[73] For
those who have made a faith-decision Christ has become wisdom,
righteousness, sanctification, and redemption (1 Cor. 1.30), but Paul
teaches that 'the rulers of this age, who are doomed to pass away'
(2.6) continue on the scene. He puts it this way: 'If our gospel is
veiled, it is veiled only to those who are perishing (ἀπολλύμενοι).
That is, the god of this world has blinded the minds of the unbelievers, to keep them from seeing the light of the gospel of the glory of
Christ' (2 Cor. 4.3, 4).

Thus, Paul speaks of two ways of knowing. What separates them
is the turn of the ages, the eschatological event of the cross. By his
work of salvation (σταυρός) and the preaching of it, God has already
characterized worldly wisdom as foolishness (1 Cor. 1.20-21). The
Jews who demanded signs saw no evidence of the miraculous in the
cross, and the gentiles who sought salvation through worldly wisdom
saw the cross as folly. But those who received the call of the gospel
discovered the cross to be the power and the wisdom of the coming
age. It is a wisdom that the unspiritual person (ψυχικός) cannot receive, but it is known by the truly 'spiritual' person (πνευματικός,
2.14-16). Those who believe are enlightened by the Spirit to see the
event of the cross as salvific.

> At the juncture of the ages is where the word of the cross is folly
> to those perishing and is the wisdom of God to those who are
> being saved. However, those who are being saved have not yet
> received all the wisdom of heaven. As Paul reminds the Corinthi-
> ans: As for knowledge it will pass away. For our knowledge is im-
> perfect … but when the perfect comes, the imperfect will pass
> away. For now, we see in a mirror dimly, but then face to face. Now
> I know in part; then I shall understand fully (13.9-12).

---

[72] ἀπολλύμενοι and σωζόμενοι are linear in force. Dieter Georgi, *Die Gegner Des
Paulus im 2 Korintherbrief Studien zur religosen Propaganda in der Spätantike* (Wissen-
schaftliche Monographien zum Alten und Neuen Testament 11; Neukirchen-
Vluyn: Neukirchener Verlag, 1964), p. 225, feels that this conceptualization is from
apocalyptic. Conversely, Ulrich Luz in *Das Geschichtsverständnis Des Paulus* (München:
Chr. Kaiser Verlag, 1968), p. 256, notes that there are parallels in both Gnostic and
apocalyptic texts.
[73] Héring, *The First Epistle of Saint Paul to the Corinthinas*, p. 10

While they do not live entirely in the new age, they know in a partial manner. For them the fundamental epistemological antithesis is not between κατὰ σάρκα and κατὰ πνεῦμα but as Martyn puts it so aptly:

> It is clear that the implied opposite of knowing κατὰ σάρκα is not knowing κατὰ πνεῦμα but rather knowing κατὰ σταυρόν. He who recognizes his life to be God's gift at the juncture of the ages recognizes also that until he is completely and exclusively in the new age, his knowing κατὰ σταυρόν. For until the *parousia*, the cross is and remains the epistemological crisis. The essential failure of the Corinthians consists in their inflexible determination to live … after the cross rather than in the cross.[74]

Ethical Dualism: A Struggle of Flesh and Spirit

In the new eschatological time, the old age is still present and has not been destroyed completely. This is seen in the quality of life manifested in the Christian community. The Christian has been renewed in a sense but has not been taken out of the old age. For Paul Christian existence during the interval that the ages overlap is a dual one. This brings into focus the moral and spiritual difference between the two ages rather than a time distinction common in apocalyptic Judaism. What the old age calls folly – the new age calls wisdom. What is power in the old age – in the new age is weakness. What is weakness in the old age is strength in the new age (1.26-28). 'This age', including the ethical and the social conditions that remained unchanged by the coming of Christ, is under the rulers of its own (2.6, 8; cf. 2 Cor. 4.4) and remains an effective force in the Christian community.

This is seen in the fact that humans are flesh (σάρξ). As σάρξ they are subject to the weaknesses and tribulations of mortality (7.28; cf. 2 Cor. 4.11) and are destined to pass away as this age will pass. Paul does not strictly identify σάρξ with the demonic powers nor designate it specifically as sinful. It is depicted in 1 Cor. 1.26 as neutral: Not many are called who were σοφοὶ κατὰ σάρκα. Presumably there were a few in the community wise according to human categories and according to the wisdom of God. The neutrality of σάρξ makes it

---

[74] J. Louis Martyn, 'Epistemology at the Turn of the Ages', *Christian History and Interpretation: Studies Presented to John Knox* (ed. W.R. Farmer, *et al.*; Cambridge: Cambridge University Press, 1967), p. 285.

possible for the two spheres to co-exist. Thus, the two are not mutu-
ally exclusive.

However, σάρξ is capable of becoming an aggressive opponent
of the power and wisdom of God. Under the power of sin (Rom.
7.14, 25) and in trying to establish its own ends (Gal. 5.16, 17), σάρξ
becomes a beachhead for sin's operations and a tyrant, holding the
human in bondage to the demonic powers of 'this age'. Schweizer
observes,

> In I Cor. 2.6, 3.18f. this aeon or κόσμος can be used for what is
> called σάρξ in I Cor. 1.2. The demonic spiritual powers belong to
> the realm of the σάρξ … Again, in I Cor. 1.24-26 the wisdom of
> God is contrasted with that of σάρξ (cf. II Cor. 1.12) and in II
> Cor. 10.4 the power of God is the antithesis of σαρκικὰ ὅπλα.[75]

When it submits to sin and gives its allegiance to the demonic powers
of this age, σάρξ stands in opposition to the will and purpose of
God. The works of σάρξ in the Christian community, where the new
age has broken into the old, are the basis for Paul's describing the
Corinthians as σάρκινοι and σαρκικοί (3.1-2).

Paul contrasts 'spiritual men' (πνευματικοί) with the 'unspiritual
men' (ψυχικοί, 2.14-16) and with 'men of the flesh' (σαρκικοί, 3.1-
2). On the one hand, the ψυχικοί are people who live without the
Spirit of God and are dominated by the life of σάρξ. On the other
hand, the σαρκικοί are people who have received the Spirit, but they
substitute the wisdom of this age for the wisdom of God and act as
though they have not the Spirit. Their deficiency is moral and ethical.
In contrast to the πνευματικοί neither the ψυχικοί nor the σαρκικοί
are led by the Spirit. The reality of sin is discerned daily in the church
(5.1-2; 6.1-2). However, Christ inaugurated a new mode of existence,
because Christians have been consecrated and become upright by the
power of Christ (6.11). Thus, at the juncture of the ages Christian
existence is a struggle of flesh (old age) and spirit (new age). Reck-
oning with this Paul perceived that the Christian lives in two ages.
The new age which is not wholly spontaneous and is in dialectical
tension with the old. Christians finds themselves in the new age
through faith, but they are exhorted to live out their new lives in the

---

[75] Eduard Schweizer, 'σάρξ', *TDNT*, VII, p. 128.

setting of the old unredeemed world (7.17-18). The enthusiasts ex-
aggerated the present power of the Christian life, but Paul understood that Christian community in Corinth existed at the turn of two
ages. So, in it were present the powers of this age that create strife
and jealousy as well as the powers of the new age that create love and
humility in a person's heart. The Christian life finds its perfection
only in what Paul calls the *parousia*.[76]

An Eschatological Phenomenon: Love

In 1 Corinthians 13, Paul notes that at the turning point of the ages
the Christians have a partial knowledge that will be done away, but
they also possess something unchangeable – love (ἀγάπη, 1 Corinthians 13). For Paul love is the distinguishing mark of the new existence. It is with this thought in mind that he can associate faith and
hope with love: Νυνὶ δὲ μένει πίστις, ἐλπίς, ἀγάπη (13.13). A puz-
zle raised by this verse is the use of μένει. It is generally thought to
be in contrast to πίπτει of 13.8 and to include a future sense. When
the charismatic gifts pass away, love, faith, and hope will continue.[77]
The ambiguity is heightened by the Νυνὶ δέ. Héring sees no sense in
speaking of the adversative use. 'All the same it would be strange to
use it in speaking of the eternal permanence of agape in the future.'[78]
Allo argues that νυνί is an adverb of time,[79] but Lietzmann takes the
νυνί logically rather than chronologically since faith, hope, and love
abide.[80] In concluding his summary of the interpretation of chapter
13, Sanders notes:

> Those who have taken the νυνί δέ here to be logical rather than
> temporal surely have the more convincing argument, for the point
> of vv. 8-13 is, of course, that those aspects of existence in which

[76] Paul's expectation of the imminent *parousia* determines his ethical admonitions in 1 Cor. 7.24-31.
[77] Héring, *The First Epistle of Saint Paul to the Corinthians*, p. 143. Wendland, *Die
Briefe an die Korinthor*, p. 107, perceives that 13.3 is a polemic-against Gnosticism
since Gnostics at Corinth were deprecating and destroying faith and hope.
[78] Héring, *The First Epistle of Saint Paul to the Corinthians*, p. 143.
[79] Ernest-Bernard Allo, *Saint Paul: prèmiere épître aux Corrinthiens* (Paris: Librairie
Lecoffre, 1956), p. 350.
[80] Hans Lietzmann, *An die Korinther I, II* (Handbuch zum Neuen Testament 9;
Tübingen: J.C.B. Mohr, 1949), p. 65.

the Corinthians place their confidence will not abide; but they certainly will exist.[81]

Therefore, as Sanders concludes, vv. 10, 11, and 13 look to the *parousia*. But Paul brings in faith and hope, when in vv. 2 and 7 he implies that they would not last until the *parousia*. Much, therefore, can be said for understanding Chapter 13 as eschatological, but it is an eschatology that has implications for Christian existence where the ages meet as well as for the future condition of the Christian.[82] The principal concern in 1 Corinthians is with 'the temporal life of the believers',[83] as evidenced by the manner in which Paul relates ἀγάπη to the issues at hand.[84] For instance, he answers the enthusiastic point of view that anything is permissible. Freedom to eat meat used in pagan worship is curbed by the Christian out of a loving concern for the weaker brother whose conscience may be wounded (8.1-2) and out of greater regard for the edification and salvation of others than for seeking his own advantage (10.23-24). The freedom to exercise the charismatic gifts, such as *glossolalia* and prophecy, is to be controlled by love so that the Christian community is built up in harmony and unity and public worship edifies all (chaps. 12, 13). It is ἀγάπη that excels and outlasts the pneumatic gifts that are vaunted by the enthusiasts.

For Paul love is something already taking place, but he recognizes that in this age humans love imperfectly. His admonition to the Corinthians is 'Make love your aim' (14.1). Nevertheless, 'in I Cor. 13, love is the link which binds limited earthly experience with the full vision of that which is to come'.[85] Love is not reserved for the future.

---

[81] Jack Sanders, 'First Corinthians 13: Its Interpretation Since the First World War,' *Interpretation* 20 (1966), p. 186.

[82] Bultmann speaks of love as an eschatological phenomenon that transplants people into eschatological existence and that it is designated thus by the fact that it is the primary form of the Spirit. *Theology of the New Testament*, I, p. 344.

[83] Sanders, 'First Corinthians 13: Its Interpretation Since the First World War', p. 178.

[84] Nils Johansson, '1 Corinthians XIII and 1 Corinthians XIV', *New Testament Studies* 10 (1964), pp. 387-92, maintains that chapter 13 describes Christ and his work and that it is the 'figure of Christ in the gospel tradition'. He observes also that ἐν ἀγάπη an ἐν (τῷ) Χριστῷ are often used in the same sense in the Pauline epistles. Cf. Rom. 13.14 and Col. 2.7.

[85] R.P. Casey, 'Gnosis, Gnosticism and the New Testament', in *The Background of the New Testament and Its Eschatology* (ed. W.D. Davies and David Daube; Cambridge: Cambridge University Press, 1964), p. 73.

It exists in this age along with faith, hope, and pneumatic qualities. Based on the Christ-event as the turning point of the two ages it is the mark and mode of Christian existence. It is the believer's experience of the transcendent in this age.[86] The old aeon, characterized by sin and death, continues, but the new age that operates through love penetrates the former. Believers live on the frontiers of two ages. This conditions their existence as a dialectical tension between the 'already-not yet'. When God finally consummates his purpose (15.24), the τὸ τέλειον ('totality' which in context here is love)[87] is expected by Paul to be fully realized and the partial abolished (13.10).

The Urzeit-Endziet Scheme

Adam-Christ Typology
Fundamental to Paul's perspective is the two-aeon scheme and especially the *Urzeit-Endzeit* idea in the view that assumes a correspondence between the End and the Beginning.[88] Under the influence of the *Urzeit-Endzeit* conception Paul's view of history focuses on the beginning points and the end point. In Pauline thought the Christ event is the end point. This appears in 1 Cor. 15.45-50, in which the first Adam and the last Adam are compared and contrasted. History is viewed under the epochs of Adam and Christ, and the stress falls on the antithetical relationship of the two epochs.[89]

---

[86] Sanders, 'First Corinthians 13: Its Interpretation Since the First World War', p. 184, says,

> Paul is in I Corinthians 13 attempting to give expression to the transcendence of *agape*. He does this first by stating that *agape* is the resurrection aspect of existence (verse 8a); but then he relates this to his opponents in terms of futuristic eschatology, so that he at the end must express the transcendence of *agape* in terms of its 'abiding.' Even here, however, the existential meaning of *agape* is expressed by the 'greatest,' so that it is seen that *agape* is primarily not a trait of human character which survives the *eschaton*, but is, rather, the transcendent which from time to time occurs within the sphere of the finite.

[87] Barrett, *The First Epistle to the Corinthians*, p. 306.

[88] T.W. Manson, *The Teaching of Jesus* (Cambridge: Cambridge University Press, 1935), p. 247, n. 2, observes that 'the two epochs (Urzeit and Endzeit) correspond because the purpose of God, which runs through and determines the whole process, is one and homogenous throughout. The end answers to the beginning because all things are in the hands of God who sees the end from the beginning.'

[89] Paul assumes two different ages; each has its origin in one man. The old is represented by Adam and the new is headed by Christ. In this passage Paul's interest is not in cosmological relationships but in an eschatological situation. If Christ is pre-existent (10.4) and the agent of creation (8.6), he was before Adam in time in terms of cosmology. Thus, Adam was not the first Adam. C.T. Craig correctly

Of course, chapter 15 deals with the question of the believer's resurrection. Prompted by the eschatological extremism of his opponents Paul discusses questions related to the mode and the nature of the believer's resurrection in vv. 35-44. In v. 44 reference is made to σῶμα ψυχικόν and the σῶμα πνευματικόν. To provide a basis for understanding the two adjectives ψυχικός πνευματικός, in v. 45 Paul describes Adam as ψυχὴ ζῶσα and Christ as πνεῦμα ζωοποιοῦν. The two are treated as representatives.[90] Adam is a ὁ ψυχικός and Christ is ὁ πνευματικός. What began as a contrast between the 'psychical' and 'pneumatic' body is broadened to include persons who represent others (v. 45).[91] However, the scope of the contrast begins to he enlarged in v. 46 where it is stated that the ψυχικός is first rather than the πνευματικός. The two terms here are comprehensive denoting two antithetical orders of existence whose sequence is stated specifically.[92] One order follows the other. The two together are cosmic in scope and encompass the whole of history. The psychical order is the epoch of Adam; it is the unredeemed world in which old humanity lives. The pneumatic order is the epoch of the last Adam; it is the new age in which the eschatological humanity share.

This cosmic, antithetical orientation is further seen in the use of the terms γή and οὐρανός (v. 47). These cosmological concepts exhibit the comprehensive, all-embracing antithesis. In v. 45, Adam and Christ are described respectively as ψυχὴ ζῶσα and πνεῦμα ζωοποιοῦν, but Paul goes on to depict the former as 'out of earth' (ἐκ γῆς) and the latter 'out of heaven' (ἐκ οὐρανοῦ).[93] Both nouns

---

observes, 'That which is related to *psyche* came first; *pneuma* comes only through the one who gives the eschatological gift'. *The First Epistle of the Corinthians*, p. 247. Thus, it seems that Paul is thinking of two orders of existence which is closely connected with the Pauline concept of the two ages.

[90] Paul treats Adam and Christ as corporate persons (cf. Rom. 5.12-21).

[91] In v. 45 Paul uses Gen. 2.7 and expands it by adding πρῶτος and Ἀδάμ. Ur-Adam speculations were commonly accepted in Judaism. Philo built his interpretation of Judaism on the conception of two kinds of people: heavenly and earthly. It is possible that Paul knew of Philo's philosophical interpretation of Judaism and is reacting here to the implications of Ur-Adam speculations. See Barrett, *The First Epistle to the Corinthians*, pp. 374-75.

[92] Barrett, *The First Epistle to the Corinthians*, pp. 374-75.

[93] 'The second man from heaven' is understood in terms of the *parousia* rather than the incarnation. It is difficult ot refrain from associating this with the whole *Son of Man* concept, especially in Daniel and 1 Enoch. Further indication of this is the mention of the kingdom in v. 50.

after the preposition ἐκ are anarthrous and thus qualitative in force signifying that one is 'earthly' and the other 'heavenly'.[94] Adam, the man of dust (χοικός, v. 48) is earthly. Christ, the one expected to come again at the *parousia*, is heavenly (ἐπουράνιος, v. 48). These represent two orders of existence – the old earthly order and the heavenly eschatological order. Furthermore, those associated with Adam belong to the earthly order, but those associated with Christ belong to the heavenly order. Those that are in union with ὁ χοικός have his image and belong to the same earthly order of beings. Those united with ὁ ἐπουράνιος belong to the race of heavenly people and will be conformed completely to his image at the time of the resurrection (v. 49).

Consequently, the resurrection of the believer is explained in terms of union with and conformity to Christ, the last Adam. He became the πνεῦμα ζωοποιοῦν and stands as the counterpart of the first Adam, the ψυχὴ ζῶσα. Adam and Christ represent two contrasting orders of life, two ages or more specifically the *Urzeit-Endzeit*. One is psychical and earthly, and the other pneumatic and heavenly. The latter is headed by Christ which is the Christian's hope of eschatological humanity.[95] Now the believer possesses eternal life in a sense, but it remains a gift hoped for.

Restoration of the Original

Unity of Humankind and Creation
Davies observes that 'it was generally recognized that the Messianic age would correspond to the beginning of all things'.[96] As we have noted, apocalyptic envisions the messianic era as a time when primeval conditions would be restored. Paul's own eschatological outlook is shaped by this expectation.

Because of the Christ-event, Paul believed that he was living in the *Endzeit* when the old aeon with its powers of sin and death were passing away and the new aeon was dawning. For Paul the cosmos had come under the dominion of sin and death, but the death and

---

[94] Friedrich Blass and Alberet Debrunner, *A Greek Grammar of the New Testament and other Early Christian Literature* (trans. and rev. Robert W. Funk; Chicago: The University of Chicago Press, 1961), p. 132.

[95] Paul expects eschatological humanity to be superior to the old: (1) eternal life (1 Cor. 15.23-24); (2) glory (15.43); (3) a spiritual body (15.50).

[96] Davies, *Paul and Rabbinic Judaism*, p. 39.

resurrection of Christ terminated the reign of these and was restoring conditions that corresponded to the primeval epoch. God's action in Christ is directed towards the new creation.[97]

A fundamental characteristic of the new creation is what Käsemann calls 'transvaluation of all values in the time of the End',[98] which is exemplified in 1 Cor. 1.26-28. From the foolish, weak, base, and despised in the world God was creating a new people. Unlike the old humanity in the new people the values of the new creation are disclosed: Christ crucified is the power and the wisdom of God for them; their earthly life is determined by the Spirit from God, not 'the spirit of the world'. So, they find life ἐν χριστῷ and the renewal of creation among them is in process (3.18; cf. 1.18). Davies reminds us that the church:

> is destined to inaugurate the eschatological unity which is to undo the divisive forces of the world. The present world is divided by the opposition between God and idols, Israel and the Gentiles, God and Satan, but all these forms of opposition are overcome in Christ, and, because Christians are one with Him, in the Church: the Church is to restore the broken unity of the universe.[99]

From Paul's perspective the unity in the church is the restoration of the original unity of humankind and creation. The distinctions between circumcised (Jew) and uncircumcised (Gentile) and the slave and free remain but have no fundamental relevance (7.17-24). The unity of the race belongs to original orders of creation. Moreover, eschatological unity restores the primeval unity of humankind. As in apocalyptic Paul links the believer's renewal with the hope that the cosmos will be redeemed from its present state. The form (σχῆμα) of this world is passing away and this is expected to give way to the new world or to a new σχῆμα (7.31; cf. Rom. 8.18-23).

The Creator continues his work even though his creatures have fallen, and his sovereignty has been challenged by evil powers. Through the Christ-event God is dispossessing the cosmic powers of the authority that they have seized in the cosmos. The divine work is to be 'consummated in the final resurrection and the new creation

---

[97] Käsemann, *New Testament Questions of Today*, p. 181.
[98] Käsemann, *New Testament Questions of Today*, p. 99.
[99] Davies, *Christian Origin and Judaism*, p. 22.

(15.20-28). The new creation begins with the resurrection of Christ which includes the restoration of all things to their primeval integrity and even to a higher state (15.21, 22).[100] The enthusiasts thought that the new creation was already complete. To the contrary, Paul understood that in his time believers still participated in both the old and new creation.

The Expectation of the Eschatological Triumph of God

Judgment-Motif and the Sacraments

In Paul's thought a connection exists between the sacraments and judgment. This connection is seen in 1 Cor. 10.1-11. After noting in vv. 1-4 that the Israelites under Moses passed through the Red Sea and received baptism and spiritual food and drink, Paul says that with most of them God was not pleased (v. 5). The basis for this is that most of them perished in the wilderness without seeing the promise land. Because of disobedience divine judgment came upon them after they received sacramental grace (vv. 6-11). Understanding that Israel's history corresponds with and has meaning for the end-time, Paul uses an event from the history of Israel to warn the Corinthians. To express this he says, 'Now these things are warnings (τύποι) for us' (v. 6). Then he adds a similar idea: 'Now these things happened to them as a warning (τυπικῶς) but they were written down for our instruction, upon whom the end of the ages has come' (v. 11). 'Israel's history is regarded as being in some sense prefigurative of the new age.'[101] God's manifestations of grace and his judgments on sin as Israel went out of Egypt are understood to be an indication of his dealing with the end-time community. The new eschatological Israel (the church) was not yet beyond sin and its consequences.

To counterbalance the claims of his opponents that baptism had brought them full salvation already, Paul maintains that in light of the Exodus event they are not beyond the possibility of judgment.[102]

---

[100] C.K. Barrett, *The First Epistle to the Corinthians*, p. 352, comments on these verses: 'Christ's act of grace and righteousness, which more than counterbalances Adam's transgression, is described in Rom. 5, and is presupposed here'.

[101] A.J. Banstra, 'Interpretation in 1 Corinthians 10.11', *Calvin Theological Journal* 6 (1971), p. 17. The precise meaning of τύποι and τυπικῶς is debatable. Some insist on the 'paranetic' sense and translate τύπος 'example' or 'pattern'. Others maintain that it has a more technical meaning of 'prerepresentation'. See pp. 14-17.

[102] See Käsemann, *New Testament Questions of Today*, pp. 125-26.

C.F.D. Moule discerns that the presence of judgment in baptism makes a distinction between judgment revealed in baptism and realized in Eucharist. Baptismal judgment is absolute and unrepeatable; eucharistic is repeated.[103] Roetzel argues that divine wrath was revealed in the cross,[104] and that those who accept Christian baptism are baptized into the judgment of the cross. From this, some at Corinth could have thought that the absolute and unrepeatable judgment of baptism was the final judgment.[105] If they had 'died with Christ' and left death behind, 'They could not understand the Eucharist as a repeated proclamation of the Lord's death (judgment) until his coming again (victory)'.[106]

In 1 Cor. 11.17-34 Paul attempts to show that God's judgment is evident in the present among them and is expected on the final eschatological day. By their individualistic (v. 21) and status-conscious conduct (v. 22), the Corinthians were destroying the unity and fellowship of the Eucharist. Anyone who had been guilty of destroying the meaning of this meal by eating and drinking in an unworthy manner (described in vv. 18-22) was doing no less than eating and drinking his way to a judgment (v. 29).[107] They were liable for this judgment from the Lord whom their unworthy action offended. Evidence of its present realization was the physical maladies that were coming on some for their misuse of the Supper (v. 30). Paul reminds them that every celebration of the Eucharist connects them to the Christ of calvary until the *parousia* (v. 26).[108]

The sacraments belong to the period in which this age and the age to come run concurrently. They put the believer in contact with the power of the future, but they stand between the death of Jesus

---

[103] C.F.D. Moule, 'The Judgement Theme in the Sacraments', in *The Background of the New Testament and its Eschatology*, pp. 464-68.

[104] Roetzel, *Judgement in the Community*, pp. 78-83.

[105] Roetzel, *Judgement in the Community*, p. 142. The intimate connection between the cross and the sacrament of baptism is made clear by Paul's questions: 'Was Paul crucified for you? Or were you baptized in the name of Paul?' (1 Cor. 1.13).

[106] Roetzel, *Judgement in the Community*, p. 142.

[107] The purpose of the words μή διακρίνων τό σῶμα was to encourage the Corinthians to restore their corporate consciousness, but scholarly opinion is divided on their specific nuance.

[108] Käsemann, 'Essays on New Testament Themes', p. 123, contends, 'Throughout the whole letter the Enthusiasts are being belaboured with two hard facts – the *Cross* and the *Parousia* (which involves the Judgement). Both are encountered in the *sacrament* in the closest proximity to each other.'

(judgment) and the *parousia* (judgment). So, in terms of Pauline es-chatology, divine justice comes into operation in the present as well as in the last day and the believers are seen '... as traveling toward the *Parousia* and therefore toward the final judgment'.[109]

Day of the Lord

Salvation is something already in progress (1 Cor. 1.18; 15.2) in the period between the Christ-event and the *parousia*, but unlike his en-thusiastic opponents Paul believed that the old age with its powers was present and would endure until the final triumph of God. He envisioned the imminent *parousia* of Christ which would bring the final judgment and full salvation (1.8; 3.13; 4.5).[110]

Paul equates Christ's *parousia* with 'the day of the Lord', a day of judgment and salvation and a prominent apocalyptic concept. It is both contemporized in his thought, and it is still outstanding.[111] In expressing the expectation of the coming judge he speaks of 'the revealing of our Lord Jesus Christ; who will sustain you to the end, guiltless in the day of our Lord Jesus Christ' (1.7, 8).[112] On that day, each person's work will be revealed for what it really is. The apoca-lyptic fires of judgment will test the quality of all work. What is of lasting value will survive this final catastrophe (3.10, 15).[113] Moreover, Paul says that he does not judge himself but reserves judgment for the Lord, who in the day of judgment will bring to light all that is

---

[109] Käsemann, 'Essays on New Testament Themes', p. 123

[110] For Paul the *parousia* is fundamental to the achievement of that 'face to face' communion (1 Cor. 13.12). In the present, fellowship is real but limited. It is a seeing 'in a mirror dimly' (13.12).

[111] In Rom. 1.18, Paul understands that God's wrath is a present reality (cf. 1 Thess. 2.16). At the same time, he speaks of it as a future possibility (Rom. 2.5-6). 2 Thessalonians 2.1 warns the reader not to believe any report 'to the effect that the day of the Lord has come'. God's ultimate purpose awaits fulfillment.

[112] In apocalyptic fashion, Paul anticipates that the saints will have a part in the final judgment. There are hints in 1 Corinthians 6, which some feel to be from a reference to a previous letter, that Paul has already used apocalyptic imagery in his eschatological teaching. Verses 2, 3 and 9 of chapter 6 speak of the saints' judging the world and the angels, and state that none but the righteous shall inherit the Kingdom. In chapter 15 this is expanded (cf. Dan. 7.22; 1 Enoch 1.9).

[113] There is in 3.13 the phrase, ἐν πυρὶ ἀποκαλύπτεται (The day 'is revealed in fire'). 'This is a common use of the present tense to indicate that a coming event is so certain that it may be spoken of as already here.' Robertson and Plummer, *A Critical and Exegetical Commentary on the first Epistle of St. Paul to the Corinthians*, p. 63. The concept ἡμέρα, as used in 1 Cor. 1.8; 3.13, is purely future and eschatological and will dawn at the *parousia* of Christ.

hidden. 'Then every man will receive his commendation from God' (4.3-5; cf. 6.9-11; 9.27; 10.1-12; 11.32).[114]

Paul believes that the *parousia* or 'the day of the Lord' is significant to the ultimate fulfillment of God's purpose. In 1 Corinthians it marks the abolishment of the last of the powers, the redemption of the body and the final triumph of God. Christ is already victor and Lord, but the struggle between the cosmic powers and the church continue until the Lord's return from heaven. At that time Paul expects the final subjection of all hostile powers[115] including death, 'the last enemy' (15.24-26).[116] Christ had overcome the power of death through his resurrection. Moreover, Paul experienced the life-giving power of Spirit in the present, but he does not expect death to be eliminated until the *parousia*. In anticipation of its abolishment he declares 'death is swallowed up in victory' (15.54).[117]

When 'the last enemy' is abolished, there is to be a transformation of believers (15.42-55). This event includes those that are to be raised from the dead (15.42-44) and those still alive at the *parousia* (15.51-5). It is to bring about a radical change. The resurrected body is imperishable, glorious, powerful, and spiritual (15.42, 43). It is celestial rather than terrestrial (15.40).[118] According to Paul, humanity is now

---

[114] It must be noted that Paul does not speculate regarding the nature of the rewards. He is satisfied to speak of rewards in such terms as ἔπαινος (1 Cor. 4.5), μισθός (3.14), and βασιλεία (6.9, 10). He does describe the βασιλεία as 'power' (4.20). Significant is the absence of any concerned effort by Paul to define these concepts. These categories used to describe 'rewards' that await the righteous 'show that the apostle's objective is to emphasize man's status as servant of a sovereign God'. Furnish, *Theology and Ethics in Paul*, p. 121.

[115] As in apocalyptic thought Paul sees evil in its cosmic dimensions. It is not so much the judgment of the individual sinner, but the abolishment of the powers that make this age evil. Paul's view is that the eradication of the powers is essential to the full realization of the age to come.

[116] The Revised Standard Version renders the verb καταργέω in these verses as 'destroy'. It literally means 'make ineffective, powerless, idle,' but it may mean 'abolish, wipe out' (*BAG*, p. 418). See Werner Foerster, 'ἐχθρός', *TDNT*, II, p. 814, for a discussion of eath as a cosmic hostile power to humanity.

[117] This statement is found also in Isa. 25.8, which is in an apocalyptic context. There will be no more death – a return to primeval conditions before the entrance of sin into the world.

[118] It does not appear that Paul thought of the resurrection body as resurrected flesh or a transformed physical body, even though there would be some sort of indissoluble link between the earthly, physical body and the celestial, spiritual body. There are quite a number of passages in apocalyptic literature which are redolent of Paul's view and from which he undoubtedly drew. The 'spiritual' bodies of the resurrected righteous are likened to 'garments of light' or 'garments of glory' (2

'the image and glory of God' (11.7). Due to Adam's fall, humanity finds itself in a state of weakness and mortality (15.22-28, 45-49). However, at the *parousia* the believer is to 'bear the image of the man of heaven' (15.49)[119] and to receive the gift of life in its ultimate sense.

The perfect and definitive salvation is expected to be realized when Christ subjects all things to himself. Christ had triumphed over the hostile powers; but, contrary to his enthusiastic opponents, the Apostle believed that Christ's subjecting (ὑποτάσσω) of all things to himself was still outstanding (15.25-26).[120] When this is accomplished, then God is to become all in all (15.28). Paul lived in the messianic kingdom but envisioned life in the final kingdom of God (15.50-54). For him eschatological subjection has been in process since Easter and the apocalyptic end is imminent. In the end 'God may be everything to everyone' (15.28), and the believer is finally brought to a state of freedom by the absolute triumph of God.

Ezra 2.39, 45; 1 Enoch 62.15, 16); the righteous are 'resplendent' and dwell in 'shining light' (1 Enoch 108.11, 12). If Dan. 12.3 is referring to the resurrected righteous ones, there is a further parallel with Paul's thought; they shall 'shine like the brightness of the firmament and like the stars for ever and ever' (cf. 1 Cor. 15.41). See S.H. Hooke, 'Life After Death V: Israel and the After-Life', *Expository Times* 76 (1965), pp. 236-39 for a discussion of the development of the belief of life after death in pre-monarchic and early monarchic periods of Israel's history. He observes that as the prophetic attitude which was firmly rooted in history began to yield to the apocalyptic view the idea of the resurrection as a feature of Jewish eschatology began to emerge.

[119] Here Paul reserves the 'image of Christ' for the *parousia* but in 2 Cor. 3.18 it is experienced presently by the believer.

[120] There are two basic contextual usages of ὑποτάσσω in the New Testament. Most frequently the verb is used in an ethical context, but only in the middle voice. Included here are those parenetic passages in which the hearer is urged to submit to the authority or jurisdiction of another. Ὑποτάσσω in the active voice occurs only in four other passages in the New Testament: 1 Cor. 15.27, 28, Eph. 1.22, Heb. 2.5-8, and Phil. 3.21. All of these are either quotations or allusions to Ps. 8.7, and the context is cosmic rather than ethical. The object of the verb in these passages is always τὰ πάντα (κτίσις) and the subject is either God (1 Cor. 15.27-28, Eph. 1.22, Hab. 2.5-6) or Christ (Phil. 3.21).

Conclusions and Implications

Much effort has been devoted to identifying apocalyptic parallels in Paul, but the determination of how basic apocalypticism is to his thought remains a New Testament problem. This study has considered only one of Paul's letters, 1 Corithians, in light of the apocalyptic doctrine of the two ages. While the conclusions that we draw will rest on our study of Jewish apocalypticism and 1 Corinthians, this work also has implications for Pauline research.

Conclusions

The foregoing study establishes that Paul's thought in 1 Corinthians stands in both continuity and discontinuity with Jewish apocalyptic. Paul's entire scheme is conditioned by his belief in the two ages. The idea of 'this age' and the 'age to come' dominates the messianic expectation in apocalyptic thought. Paul shared the view with apocalyptic that the present age is evil and temporary and is now in process of passing away and that the age to come is the messianic age. But this dichotomy is not very precise in 1 Corinthians. Paul realistically depicts this age as evil; but in contrast to the form of apocalyptic that sees the mighty hand of God in remote events of the past and limits the demonstration of the powers of the new age to the end of this age, he teaches that the new age dawns in the Christ-event. It is now the time of salvation, for Jesus Christ, the Messiah, has come already and Christ is now Lord. Consequently, Paul builds on the antithetical structure of Jewish apocalyptic, but he reshapes it so that God's sovereignty and redemptive activity are in process of realization. The new world of apocalyptic expectation is somehow already present; but refusing to follow the enthusiasts, he insists the old age has not passed away entirely. The dualistic view of history that stresses a radical temporal discontinuity between, 'this age' and the coming age and that relegates the kingdom of God exclusively to the future is modified by the Christ-event. The Pauline present is a time in which the ages overlap. The extreme dualism common in Jewish apocalypticism is subdued in 1 Corinthians. The central declaration of the Pauline Gospel is that God's eschatological act in Christ made the future concomitant and contemporaneous with the present.

As we have noted, the present age for Paul is evil. It is full of distress: 'The messianic woes' herald that the end is imminent. Demonic forces are present and operative in this age. The church is engaged in eschatological combat with the evil forces in the world. Paul's view that the end is impending and that the unredeemed world is controlled by cosmic powers does not cause him to look on the present as empty and to fall into the Jewish apocalyptic preoccupation with the future. This is evident in his stress upon Christ the enthroned Lord who presently rules the church and world. The use of apocalyptic by Paul affirms rather than denies the unity of history and thus he maintains that since the future age penetrates the present the kingdom of God is relevant to and operative in 'this age'.

The presence of the Spirit in the Christian community is evidence that the power of the coming age, that is, God's transcendent power, has already broken in and fills the present with meaning. The church belongs already to the eschatological age and claims the life of the new age as a gift of the Spirit. Salvation has already been given to the church; the new eschatological power of God that raised Jesus Christ is already operative through the Spirit in the present life of the believers. What Paul says about the Spirit reflects the dialectical character of his thought. The solution to the tension in which the church lives in the present lies in the Spirit, the principal sign that the new age has dawned and the assurance that God will bring to complete fulfillment the life which the believers have received already. The basis, then, for Christian liberty and hope is not that the present world is approaching the end, but God's redemptive activity belonging to both the present and the future. The future belongs to God, and eschatological salvation is already present.

The apostle's perspective rests on the belief that this age has come to an end, and yet it continues. The age to come has moved into the present. And so, the believer exists now at the turning point of the ages. This accounts for the tension in which the church lives in the present. Accordingly, the life of the believer in this age is a dual one. Living in the time where the two ages interpenetrate, the Christian finds an antithesis between the wisdom of this age and the age to come and between flesh and Spirit. It is significant that knowledge for the Christian is not limited to human judgment as the 'natural man' (1 Cor. 2.14) is. The 'natural man' does not have the Spirit and thus is blind to the significance of what God did in Christ. By contrast, the Christian knows the mysteries of God. Such knowledge is according to the cross through the Spirit. Yet the life of the believer in the present age is marked by incompleteness with respect to knowledge and communion with God. Thus, as an inhabitant of two ages at the same time the believer exists in an ambiguous situation. The fact that his existence is characterized by the dialectic 'already-not yet' is evident also in regard to freedom in Christian living. He belongs to the new age but is not able to isolate himself from this present evil age. The presence of the evil forces of this age in the Christian community give rise to the struggle between flesh and Spirit. Flesh itself is not evil; but when it is taken over by sin, it becomes an ally of the evil powers of this age and manifest itself in the believer's disobedience to the will of God.

Though the powers of the old age create strife and jealousy within the Christian community, fundamental to the life of the people of the new age is love. Love itself is not an apocalyptic motif, but Paul takes seriously love as a quality of life that is to characterize the Christian living at the juncture of the ages. For Paul, love is eschatological. The absence of love among the Corinthians was a contradiction to the claims of the enthusiasts to eschatological fulfillment. Their lack of corporate concern revealed that they had lost consciousness of living in the time where the ages meet. By stressing the eschatological character of love, Paul limits the claims of the enthusiasts that the *eschaton* had fully arrived.

The extreme apocalyptic pessimism that defers God's saving activity to the end is absent from 1 Corinthians. Apocalyptic recognizes that history is a universal process and is ordered ultimately according to the divine plan. This Paul shared with the apocalyptists. In his First Letter to the Corinthians he views history under the epochs of Adam and Christ and makes use of the *Urzeit-Endzeit* conception in apocalyptic. Rather than seeing a historical continuity between Adam and

Christ, he stresses the antithetical relationship of the two to each other. As a number of the apocalyptists Paul traces the origin of sin back to the fall of Adam. He contends that the old aeon with Adam as its head is characterized by sin and death. The new aeon which Christ introduced and of which he is the head has set in motion a reversal of the universal effects of Adam's sin and is expected by Paul to issue ultimately into the total restoration of all things. The *Endzeit* which Paul believed to have been inaugurated by the Christ-event is to correspond to the *Urzeit* and even restore a higher state than the primeval ideal. Paul offers no sketch of epochs nor an apocalyptic timetable. This stands in contrast to some elaborate schemes that assumed that the end could be determined.

Paul does not fall into the fantasy of enthusiasm and recognizes temporal and qualitative discontinuity of the two ages. Contrary to Jewish apocalyptic his stress falls on the latter, emphasizing the moral and spiritual antithesis between the two ages; but he does teach that the transcendent power of God has not had full effect on this world. Salvation is not visibly present in its fullness. There is present the Spirit, the sign and pledge of ultimate redemption; but the hostile powers have not been abolished nor the resurrection of the dead accomplished. In a typical apocalyptic vein, Paul anticipates God's absolute transcendence over all humanity and the entire cosmos. Apart from warning the Corinthians that the times are becoming treacherous, he offers no apocalyptic speculations as to what the future turn of events may be nor a description of eschatological battles. In apocalyptic, the emphasis is consistently on the last judgment, but in 1 Corinthians it is on the cross, the ground of salvation and hope. The expectation of judgment does have its place in the letter. However, the apostle in modifying the apocalyptic scheme of the two ages maintains that the future has been brought into the present and that judgment is now being realized. 'It is precisely in the salvific deed manifest in the cross of Christ that judgment and vindication has already begun.'[1]

Similar to apocalyptic theology, Paul stresses more the corporate aspect of judgment. This is seen in the important place that he assigns the Christian community in judgment passages. He believes that the church is now and will be on the Day of the Lord an instrument

---

[1] Roetzel, *Judgement in the Community*, p. 177.

of judgment. He cautions the community against assuming that the sacraments placed them beyond future judgment. Through the sacraments judgment is both realized and anticipated. They stand between the cross (judgment) and the Day of the Lord (judgment). Contrary to much apocalyptic thought Paul does not view judgment primarily in terms of the condemnation of gentiles and apostate Jews. His concern is the Christian community. While he sees judgment in broad dimensions that include God finally calling to account those on the outside, his stress is on the ways present judgment is realized in the community.

As Paul formulates it in 1 Corinthians, eschatological recompense focuses in particular on judgment in the community, but individual concerns are not entirely absent on the day of judgment. Paul is convinced that all people are ultimately and individually accountable to God for their deeds. It is expected that on the Day of the Lord when the last of the powers is abolished that the spiritual body is to be bestowed on the believer.

In comparison with normal apocalyptic imagery of the final judgment Paul's picture is notable for its restraint, but in keeping with the general line of apocalyptic tradition Paul associates the Day of the Lord with judgment and the final triumph of God. The apocalyptists expected the demonic forces to be decisively defeated on that day. For Paul, they had already been defeated in the Christ-event but not finally abolished. The traditional view of the Day of the Lord is that it refers to a day that Yahweh or the Messiah will intervene for the holy people, Israel. It is a day of judgment for the 'nations' and God's opponents but a day of deliverance for Israel. This conception is modified by Paul. For him the 'Day of the Lord' is 'the day of the coming of our Lord Jesus' (1 Cor. 1.8) and is when the decisive victory won in the cross and resurrection is disclosed and the cosmic powers abolished. But as in apocalyptic Paul affirms that God's direct intervention can bring ultimate fulfillment of the divine purpose. He envisions the transformation of history and cosmic redemption that will bring to full actualization the power, love, righteousness, freedom, peace, and joy that the new people of God already know in Jesus Christ.

Implications

The conclusions drawn from the preceding study have some implications for understanding Pauline eschatology and redemption. In light of our examination of 1 Corinthians the work of Albert Schweitzer and Ernst Käsemann is significant. Schweitzer emphasizes the influence of Jewish apocalypticism on Paul's theology and sees the stress of Pauline thought to be on the cosmic dimension of eschatology rather than on individual salvation or inward participation in God's saving events. Making no attempt to divorce Paul from his Christian context Käsemann reemphasizes the connection between Jewish apocalyptic and Pauline eschatology. He acknowledges that the Apostle has reinterpreted the apocalyptic scheme of the two ages to serve his own theology and attempts to take into account both the realized and futuristic dimension of Paul's thought.

The specific implications of this investigation are: (1) We have demonstrated that the two-age motif is fundamental to Paul's perspective in 1 Corinthians. This supports the thesis that apocalyptic is at least one strand in Pauline thought and that research must consider the possibility that it is more fundamental to Paul's thought than assumed previously. Therefore, one area that needs further investigation is the relation of apocalyptic to the eschatology of the Pauline *corpus*. (2) The Christian perspective of Paul does not dominate his thought to the extent that apocalypticism is abandoned in 1 Corinthians. Corporate concerns are reflected in such concepts as the eschatological community, kingdom of God, and the two cosmic epochs. However, his Christian perspective was decisive in the reinterpretation of the doctrine of the two ages. So, while he uses the traditional conceptualism of apocalyptic, he demonstrates originality in his employment of the traditional forms. (3) Our study disallows any narrow conception of Pauline eschatology. For Paul, eschatology is in process and encompasses the past, present, and future. (4) If our identification of Paul's opponents is correct, he employed apocalyptic language apologetically to defend his understanding of the Christian faith against enthusiasm. This raises the question, 'Is the prominence of apocalyptic tradition in 1 Corinthians due primarily to Pauline polemics?' If so, is this a function of apocalyptic in other letters of Paul? Our investigation has not solved all the problems posed by Paul's use of apocalyptic motifs, but it does point out the fundamental importance of the two-age motif to Paul's thought in 1 Corinthians.

EXCURSUS: ON THE PROBLEM OF GNOSTICISM

One prominent issue that confronts contemporary New Testament scholarship is to understand the relationship of Gnosticism to the New Testament. Involved in this area of research are such concerns as the definition of the terms 'Gnosticism' and 'Gnostic', the quest ion of pre-Christian Gnosticism and the exegesis of the New Testament on the basis of pre-Christian Gnosticism.

The definition of Gnosticism has proved to be a difficult task since it is a term that has been used to cover a wide spectrum of religious phenomena.[1] Finding that it is impossible to reduce Gnosticism to a short definition, van Baaren lists sixteen characteristics of this religious complex.[2] According to Yamauchi, most scholars agree that fundamental to Gnosticism 'is a radical ontological dualism between the divine and the created inasmuch as creation of the world and matter has resulted from ignorance and error'.[3] Noch defines it broadly as 'a dualistic piety of redemption'[4] and Grant as 'a religion of saving knowledge'.[5]

In a broad sense there is some agreement regarding the nature of Gnosticism, but to determine where it begins and ends exactly is

---

[1] Robert M. Grant, *Gnosticism and Early Christianity* (New York: Harper and Row, 1959), p. 6. Koester also recognizes that the term Gnostic is ambiguous and vague. Cf. *Trajectories Through Early Christanity*, pp. 115-16.

[2] van Baaren, 'Toward a Definition of Gnosticism', pp. 178-80.

[3] Edwin Yamauchi, *Pre-Christian Gnosticism* (Grand Eerdmans, 1973), p. 15.

[4] Arthur D. Noch, *Early Gentile Christianity and Its Hellenistic Background* (New York: Harper and Row, 1964), p. 14.

[5] Grant, *Gnosticism and the Early Church*, p. 10. Hans Jonas, 'Delimitation of Gnostic Phenomenon Typological and Historical', *Le origini dello Gnosticismo*, p. 98, observes that in Gnosticism knowledge has a soteriological function. To the Gnostics, ignorance is neither a neutral state nor the mere absence of knowledge, but it affects the human spirit and prevents people from discovering truth for themselves.

difficult.[6] Those who define the concepts 'Gnosticism' and 'Gnostic' in broad terms tend to see Gnosticism as a pre-Christian phenomenon.[7] Those who use it with a more restrictive meaning are prone to deny that New Testament Christianity presupposes the existence of Gnosticism. As a representative of the former, Bultmann argues that Gnostic terminology is used to translate the Christian message for Hellenistic Christianity. This is carried through in detail with the conclusion that there are discernible 'Gnostic' motifs in the New Testament and that the influence of Gnosticism has a decisive influence on Paul's thought.[8] For example, in 1 Corinthians, Bultmann detects a Hellenistic-dualistic depreciation of the body in Paul's treatment of the marriage question (7.1-7). He thinks that Paul's salvation scheme is influenced by the Gnostic Redeemer-myth (2.8) and that Gnostic terminology provides him with anthropological concepts.[9]

Walter Schmithals also argues that Gnosticism is a pre-Christian phenomenon which was incorporated into Judaism in Babylon and from there into Paul. He sees in the Corinthian correspondence evidence of a Gnostic *Weltanschauung* and identifies Paul's opponents in both 1 and 2 Corinthians as Jewish Gnostics.[10] The fact that Paul does

---

[6] See Helmer Ringgren, 'Qumran and Gnosticism', *The Origin of Gnosticism* (Leiden: Brill, 1967), p. 383, says, 'In the world of ideas it is hard to draw absolute borderlines. An idea or trend of ideas may manifest itself in various ways in different milieus and still be the same, historically speaking'.

[7] The Reitzenstein-Bousset-Bultmann-Schmithals school not only sees Gnosticism as a pre-Christian movement but also as a unified phenomenon. Van Baaren, 'Toward a Definition of Gnosticism', pp. 174-75, apparently understands that Gnostic speculations are quite fluid. He is convinced that all attempts to define Gnosticism as a phenomenological complex are doomed to failure. The only way to formulate a satisfactory definition is that of considering Gnosticism as a historical complex belonging to a certain age and a certain culture.

[8] See Rudolf Bultmann, *Primitive Christianity in Its Contemporary Setting and Theology of the New Testament*, I, pp. 164-83.

[9] Bultmann, *Primitive Christianity in Its Contemporary Setting and Theology of the New Testament*, pp. 174-75 In treating 'γινώσκω,' *TDNT*, I, p. 710, Bultmann says that opposition to Gnosticism can be seen in 1 Corinthians 13. In v. 8 the use of γνῶσις on the Gnostic analogy, denotes 'a pneumatic capacity for knowledge'. The antithesis between γνῶσις and ἀγάπη is noted by the fact that γνῶσις is set under ἀγάπη and it is described by Paul as provisional and inadequate. In this life there is no relationship with God on the basis of γνῶσις. Bultmann adds, 'When Paul uses ἐπιγνώσομαι for the future relationship, he is certainly adopting Gnostic usage. But the term is robbed of its Gnostic significance by the phrase καθὼς καὶ ἐπιγνώσθην'.

[10] Schmithals, *Gnosticism in Corinth*, pp. 113-14. Some scholars contrary to Bultmann and Schmithals distinguish between Paul's opponents in 1 and 2 Corinthians.

not reject all Gnostic tendencies is construed to be an implicit approval of them. A clear example of this, according to Schmithals, is Paul's use of the antithesis of ψυχικός-πνευματικός.[11] Moreover, he attributes the formula ἀνάθεμα Ἰησοῦς (1 Cor. 12.3) to the Jewish Gnostics who had infiltrated the Church at Corinth. Supposedly they found the proclamation of the crucified Christ offensive; and reverting to their first language, Aramaic, they in ecstatic excitement cursed Jesus. For Schmithals the issue is the same in 1 Cor. 1.17-2.5 where he finds evidence of a Pauline polemic against the Gnostic opponents who proclaimed an esoteric system of knowledge and denied the importance of crucifixion.[12] In fact, Schmithals offers a thoroughgoing exposition of Paul's Christology, anthropology, sacramentalism, and eschatology in terms of either his agreements or disagreements with Jewish Gnosticism.

However, a number of scholars question the position of those who subscribe to a pre-Christian Gnostic system. R.McL. Wilson denies that a full-grown type of Gnosticism can be proven for Corinth. He sees several pre-Christian affinities to Gnosticism, especially in Jewish apocalyptic, Qumran, and Pharisaism.[13] Paul's opponents at Corinth, argues Wilson, were not fully Gnostic in the Second Century sense and, furthermore, such tendencies among the Corinthian opponents should be categorized by the broader and more vague term 'gnosis' and seen as influencing the thought in later Gnostic schools.[14] Likewise, Conzelmann doubts the existence of a mature type of Gnosticism at Corinth. The thesis that the Corinthians held a Gnostic Christology, notes Conzelmann, is refuted by the fact that Paul presupposes that they shared his confession of faith. As Ernst Käsemann and others, he describes Paul's Corinthian opponents as 'spirit enthusiasts', not as Gnostics.[15]

Georgi insists that the opponents of 2 Corinthians are not Gnostics but Hellenistic Jewish-Christian missionaries. See *Die Gegner des Paulus im 2 Korintherbrief* and Yamauchi, *Pre-Christian Gnosticism*, pp. 41-42.

[11] Schmithals, *Gnosticism in Corinth*, pp. 169-70.

[12] Schmithals, *Gnosticism in Corinth*, pp. 124-25, 135-36.

[13] See R.McL. Wilson, *Gnosis in the New Testament* (Philadelphia: Westminster Pess, 1968).

[14] R.McL. Wilson, 'How Gnostic Were the Corinthians?' *New Testament Studies* 19 (1972), pp. 65-74.

[15] Hans Conzelmann, 'On the Analysis of the Confessional Formula in I Corinthians 15.3-5', *Interpretation* 20 (1966), p. 24. Conzelmann in *A Commentary on the First Epistle to the Corinthians* (Hermeneia; trans. James W. Leitch; Philadelphia:

There are, of course, many instances in Paul's epistles when he openly reflects the temper of his time both in thought and language. Such Pauline concepts as τέλειοι, ἄρχοντες, μυστήριον, πνευματικοί, and ψυχικοί are terminology of later Gnosticism.[16] Judaism was not closed against all Hellenistic influences. However, it is the opinion of Noch that the fusion of Judaism and Greek philosophy is 'very far from affording anything like probable indications of a pre-Christian *Weltreligion*'.[17] Moreover, Quispel states that 'it remains to be proved that it (Gnosticism) is pre-Christian'.[18]

In conclusion it is well to bear in mind the following: (1) It is still widely held that Gnosticism and Gnosis were signifcant factors in the origins of Christianity.[19] (2) If we concede that Paul interacted with a rudimentary form of Gnosticism, it must be remembered that Christianity did not directly confront Gnosticism until the second century CE. Thus, we cannot afford to be too dogmatic concerning the traces of incipient Gnosticism that are in the documents of the New Testament.[20] A danger is 'that technical data and origins of forms and concepts will he explained but the meaning left unelucidated'.[21]

Fortress Press, 1975), p. 15, still maintains that 1 Corinthians does not reflect a mature kind of Gnosticism, but he does modify his earlier view by conceding that the Corinthians may be described as proto-Gnostics.

   [16] Scharlemann, *Qumran and Corinth*, p. 67.

   [17] Noch, *Early Gentile Christianity and Its Hellenistic Background*, p. xvi.

   [18] Gilles Quispel, *Gnosis als Weltreligion* (Zurich: Origo Verlag, 1951), p. 5

   [19] R.P. Casey, 'Gnosis, Gnosticism and the New Testament', *The Background of New Testament and Its Eschatology* (ed. W.D. Davies and David Daube; Cambridge: Cambridge University Press, 1964), p. 55.

   [20] Koester, *Trajectories Through Early Christianity*, p. 137, sees the crucial problem of Gnosticism as 'how to interpret early forms of Gnosticism with respect to their roots in early Christian and Jewish theology'. In this regard he thinks that the Gospel of Thomas occupies a decisive position. Noch, *Early Gentile Christianity and Its Hellenistic Background*, p. xvii, warns against taking Manichaen or Gnostic texts which quote the New Testament and using them to reconstruct a hypothetical forerunner of Christianity.

   [21] Sanders, '1 Corinthians 13: Its Interpretation Since the First World War', p. 166.

BIBLIOGRAPHY

Allo, Ernest-Bernard, *Saint Paul: premère épître aux Corinthiens* (Paris: Libraire Lecoffre, 1935).

Baird, William, 'Pauline Eschatology in Hermeneutical Perspective', *New Testament Studies* 17 (1970-71), pp. 314-27.

Banstra, A.J., 'Interpretation in 1 Corinthians 10:1-11.11', *Calvin Theological Journal* 6 (1971), pp. 5-21.

Barrett, C.K., *The First Epistle to the Corinthians* (Harper's New Testament Commentaries; New York: Harper and Row, 1968).

—*From First Adam to Last* (New York: Charles Scribner's Sons, 1962).

—*The New Testament Background* (New York: Harper and Row, 1956).

Bartels, Robert A., 'Law and Sin in 4th Edras and St. Paul', *Lutheran Quarterly* 1 (1949), pp. 319-29.

Bartsch, H.W. (ed.), *Kerygma and Myth: a Theological Debate* (trans. R. H. Fuller; New York: Harper and Row, 1961).

Batey, Richard (ed.), *New Testament Issues* (New York: Harper and Row, 1970).

Bauer, Walter, William F. Arndt, and F. Wilbur Gingrich, *A Greek English Lexicon of the New Testament and Other Early Christian Literature* (Chicago: University of Chicago Press, 1961).

Beardslee, William A., *Human Achievement and Divine Vocation in the Message of Paul* (Naperville, IL: Alec Arrenson, 1961).

—'The New Testament Apocalyptic in Recent Interpretation', *Interpretation* 25 (1971), pp. 419-35.

Berger, Klaus, 'Zu den sogenannten Satzen Geilgen Rechtes', *New Testament Studies* 17 (1970), pp. 10-40.

Bianchi, Ugo (ed.), *Le origini dello Gnosticismo* (Supplements to Numen; 7 vols.; Leiden: Brill, 1969).

Blass, Friedrick, and Albert Debrunner A., *Greek Grammar of the New Testament and Other Early Christian Literature* (trans. and rev. by Robert W. Funk; Chicago: The University of Chicago Press, 1961).

Boers, H.W., 'Apocalyptic Eschatology in I Corinthians 15: An Essay in Contemprorary Interpretation', *Interpretation* 21 (1967), pp. 50-65.

Bornkamm, Günther, *Paul* (trans. D.M.G. Stalker; New York: Harper and Row, 1971).

Bouttier, Michel, *Christianity according to Paul* (Naperville, IL: Alec R. Allenson, 1966).

Box, G.H. 'Jewish Apocalyptic in the Apostolic Age', *The Expositor* 24 (1922), pp. 321-45; 437-59.

Buck, Charles, and Greer Taylor, *Saint Paul* (New York: Charles Scribner's Sons, 1969).

Bultmann, Rudolf, *Essays Philosophical and Theological* (New York: Macmillan Company, 1955).

—'History and Eschatology in the New Testament', *New Testament Studies* 1 (1954-55), pp. 5-16.

—'Ist Apokalyptik die Mutter der christlichen Theologie?', *Apophoreta: Festschrift für Ernst Haenchen* (Berlin: Alfred Topelmann Verlag, 1964).

—*The Old and the New Man in the Letters of Paul* (trans. Keith R. Crim; Richmond: John Knox Press, 1967).

—*The Presence of Eternity: History and Eschatology* (Edinburgh: The University Press, 1957).

—*Primitive Christianity in Contemporary Setting* (trans. R.H. Fuller; New York: World Publishing Company, 1956).

—*Theology of the New Testament* (2 vols.; trans. Kendrick Grobel; New York: Charles Scribner's Sons, 1951).

Charles, R.H. (ed.) *The Apocrypha and Pseudepigrapha of the Old Testament* (2 vols.; Oxford: The Clarendon Press, 1913).

—*The Ascension of Isaiah* (London: Society for Promoting Christian Knowledge, 1915).

—'Eschatology: The Doctrine of the Future Life', in *Israel, Judaism and Christianity* (New York: Schocken Books, 1963).

Conzelmann, Hans, *A Commentary on the First Epistle to the Corinthians* (Hermeneia; trans. James W. Leitch; Philadelphia: Fortress Press. 1975).

—'On the Analysis of the Confessional formula in 1 Corinthians 15:3-5', *Interpretation* 20 (1966), pp. 15-25.

Craig, C.T., *First Epistle to the Corinthians* (Interpreter's Bible, Vol. 10; New York: Abingdon, 1954).

Cullmann, Oscar, *The Early Church* (trans. A.J.B. Higgins and Stanley Godman; Philadelphia, Westminster Press, 1966).

Dahl, Murdock E., *The Resurrection of the Body* (Naperville, IL: Alec R. Allenson, 1962).

Davies, W.D., *Christian Origins and Judaism* (Philadelphia: Westminster Press, 1962).

—*Paul and Rabbinic Judaism* (New York: Harper and Row, 1948).

Davies, W.D., and David Daube (eds.), *The Background of the New Testament and its Eschatology* (Cambridge: Cambridge University Press, 1964).

The Dead Sea Scrolls (trans. from Hebrew by Geza Vermes; New York: Harper and Row, 1964).

Dodd, C.H., *The Apostolic Preaching and Its Developments* (New York: Harper and Row, 1964).

—*New Testament Studies* (Manchester: The University Press, 1953).

—*The Parables of the Kingdom* (London: Nisbet and Company, 1935).

Ellis, E. Earle, *Paul and His Recent Interpreters* (Grand Rapids: Eerdmans, 1961).

Frost, S.B., *Old Testament Apocalyptic* (London: Epworth Press, 1952).

Fuller, Reginald H., *The Foundations of New Testament Christology* (New York: Charles Scribner's Sons, 1965).

Funk, Robert W. (ed.), *Apocalypticism* (Journal for Theology and the Church 4; New York: Herdor and Herder, 1969).

Furnish, Victor P., *Theology and Ethics in Paul* (Nashville: Abingdon, 1968).

Gale, Herbert M., *The Use of Analogy in the Letters of Paul* (Philadelphia: The Westminster Press, 1964).

Gaster, Theodore H., *The Dead Sea Scrolls* (New York: Doubleday and Company, 1956).

Georgi, Dieter, *Die Gegner des Paulus im 2 Korintherbrief: Studien zur religosen Propaganda in Spätantike* (Wissenschaftlich Monographien zum Alten and Neuen Testament 11; Neukirchen-Vluyn: Neukirchener Verlag, 1964).

Glasson, T. Francis, *Greek Influence in Jewish Eschatology* (London: SPCK, 1961).

Grant, Robert M., *Gnosticism and Early Christianity* (New York: Harper and Row, 1959).

Gunkel, Hermann, *Schöpfung und Chaos in Urzeit and Endzeit* (Göttingen: Vandenhoeck und Ruprecht, 1888).

Güttgemanns, E., *Der leidende Apostel und sein Herr* (Göttingen: Vandenhoeck und Ruprecht, 1966).

Hamilton, N.Q., *Holy Spirit and Eschatology in Paul* (Edinburgh: Oliver and Boyd, 1957).

Hanson, Paul D., 'Old Testament Apocalyptic Reexamined', *Interpretation* 25 (1971), pp. 454-78.

—'Studies in the Origins of Jewish Apocalyptic' (PhD dissertation; Harvard University, 1969).

Hennecke, Edgar (ed.), *New Testament Apocrypha* (2 vols.; ed. Wilhelm Schneemelcher; trans. and ed. R. McL. Wilson; Philadelphia: Westminster Press, 1964).

Héring, Jean, *The First Epistle of St. Paul to the Corinthians* (trans. A.W. Heathcote and P.J. Allcock; London: The Epworth Press, 1962).

Hooke, H.S. 'Life After Death V: Israel and the AfterLife', *Expository Times* 26 (1965), pp. 236-39.

Hurd, J.C., *The Origin of I Corinthians* (New York: Seabury Press, 1965).

Johansson, Hils, 'I Corinthians XIII and I Corinthians XIV', *New Testament Studies* 10 (1964), pp. 387-92.

Käsemann, Ernst, 'Die Anfänge christlicher Theologie', *Zeitschrift für Theologie und Kirche* 57 (1960), pp. 162-85.

—*New Testament Questions of Today* (trans. H.J. Montague; Philadelphia: Fortress Press, 1969).

Kennedy, Harry Argus, *St. Paul's Conception of the Last Things* (London: Hodder and Stoughton, 1904).

Kittel, Gerhard, and Gerhard Friedrich (eds.) *Theological Dictionary of the New Testament* (trans. and ed. Geoffrey W. Bromiley; 9 vols.; Grand Rapids: Eerdmans, 1964-74).

Koch, Klaus; *Ratlos vor der Apokalyptik* (Gütersloh: Gerd Mohn, 1970).

Kümmel, Werner G., *Introduction to the New Testament* (trans. A.J. Mattil, Jr.; New York: Abingdon Press, 1965).

—*The New Testament: The History of the Investigation of Its Problems* (New York: Abingdon Press: 1970).

Kwiran, Manfred, *The Resurrection of the Dead* (Basel: Friedrick Reinhardt Kommissionserlag, 1972).

Lampe, G.W., *The Seal of the Spirit* (New York: Longmans, Green and Company, 1951).

Langston, Edward, *Essentials of Demonology* (London: Epworth Press, 1949).

Lietzmann, Hans, *An die Korinther I, II* (Handbuch zum Neuen Testament 9; Tübingen: J.C.B. Mohr, 1949).

Luz, Ulrich, 'Entmythologisierung als Aufgabe der Christologie', *Evangelische Theologie* 26 (1966), pp. 349-68.

Manson, T.W., *The Teaching of Jesus* (Cambridge: Cambridge University Press, 1935).

Martyn, J. Louis, 'Epistemology at the Turn of the Ages', in W.R. Farmer, *et al.* (eds.), *Christian History and Interpretation: Studies Presented to John Knox* (Cambridge: Cambridge University Press, 1967).

Moore, George F., *Judaism in the First Centuries of the Christian Era* (3 Vols.; Cambridge: Harvard University Press, 1927).

Moule, C.R.D., 'The Influence of Circumstances on the Use of Eschatological Terms', *Journal of Theological Studies* 15 (1964), pp. 1-15.

Munck, Johannes, *Paul and the Salvation of Mankind* (trans. Frank Clark; Richmond: John Knox Press, 1959).

Murdock, William R., 'History and Revelation in Jewish Apocalyptcism', *Interpretation* 21 (1967), pp. 167-87.

Noch, Arthur D., *Early Gentile Christianity and Its Hellenistic Background* (New York: Harper and Row, 1964).

Owens, H.P., 'Eschatology and Ethics in the New Testament', *Scottish Journal of Theology* 15 (1962), pp. 369-82.

Ploeger, Otto, *Theokratie und Eschatologie* (Neukirchen: Neuenkirchener Verlag, 1959).

Quispel, Gilles, *Gnosis als Weltreligion* (Zurich: Origo Verlag, 1951).

Rad, Gerhard von, *Old Testament Theology* (trans. D.M.G. Stalker; 2 Vols.; New York: Harper and Row, 1965).

—*Wisdom in Israel* (Nashville: Abingdon Press, 1972).

Ringgren, Helmer, 'Qumran and Gnosticism'. *The Origin of Gnosticism* (Leiden: Brill, 1967).

Robertson, Archibald, and Alfred Plummer, *A Critical and Exegetical Commentary of the First Epistle of St. Paul to the Corinthians* (International Critical Commentary; Edinburgh: T. & T. Clark, 1914).

Robinson, James M., and Helmut Koester, *Trajectories through Early Christianity* (Philadelphia: Fortress Press, 1971).

Roetzel, Calvin J., *Judgment in the Community* (Leiden: Brill, 1972).

Rollins, Wayne G., 'The New Testament Apocalyptic', *New Testament Studies* 17 (1970-71), pp. 454-76.

Rowley, H.H., *The Relevance of Apocalyptic* (London: Lutterworth Press, 1947).

Russell, D.S., *The Method and Message of Jewish Apocalyptic* (Philadelphia: Westminster Press, 1964).

Sanders, Jack, '1 Corinthians 13: Its Interpretation Since the First World War', *Interpretation* 20 (1966), pp. 159-87.

Scharlemann, M.H., *Qumran and Corinth* (New York: Bookman Associates, 1962).

Schmithals, Walter, *Gnosticism in Corinth: An Investigation of the Letters to the Corinthians* (trans. John E. Steely; New York: Abingdon Press, 1971).

Schoeps, H.J., *Paul: The Theology of the Apostle in the Light of Jewish Religious History* (trans. Harold Knight; Philadelphia: Westminister Press, 1966).

Schrage, Wolfgang, 'Die Stellung zur Welt bei Paulus, Epiktet und in der Apokalyptik: ein Beitrag zu I Kor. 7:29-31', *Zeitschrift für Theologie und Kirche* 61 (1964), pp. 125-54.

Schweitzer, Albert, *The Mystery of the Kingdom of God* (trans. William Montgomery; London: A. & C. Black, 1925).

—*The Mysticism of Paul the Apostle* (trans. William Montgomery; New York: Henry Holt and Company, 1931).

—*Out of My Life and Thought* (New York: Rinehart and Winston, 1933).

—*Paul and His Interpreters* (trans. William Montgomery; New York: Macmillan Company, 1948).

Strack, Hermann, and Paul Billerbeck, *Kommentar zum Neuen Testament aus Talmud und Midrasch* (München: C.H. Beck'sche Verlagsbuchhandlung, 1926).

Thackeray, H. St. John, *The Relation of St. Paul to Contemporary Jewish Thought* (New York: Macmillan Company, 1900).

Vawter, Bruce, 'And He Shall Come Again with Glory: Paul and Christian Apocalyptic', in *Studiorum Paulinorum Congressus Internationalis Catholicus 1961* (Analecta Biblica 17-18; Rome: E. Pontificco Instituto Biblico, 1963).

Volz, Paul, *Die Eschatologie der jüdischen Gemeinde im neuntestamentlichen Zeitalter* (Tübingen: Verlag von J.C.B. Mohr, 1934).

Weiss, Johannes, 'Das Problem der Entstehung des Christentums' *Archiv für Religionswissenchaft* 16 (1913), pp. 423-515.

—*Der erste Korintherbrief* (Meyer Kommentar; Göttingen: Vandenhoeck und Ruprecht, 1910).

—*Earliest Christianity* (ed. Frederick C. Grant; 2 vols.; New York: Harper and Row, 1959).

—*Jesus' Proclamation of the Kingdom of God* (ed. L.E. Keck; trans. R.H. Heirs and D.L. Holland; Philadelphia: Fortress Press, 1971).

—*Die Predigt Jesu vom Reiche Gottes* (Göttingen: Vandenhoeck und Ruprecht, 1892).

Wendland, H.D., *Die Brief an die Korinther* (Das Neue Testament Deutsch 7; Göttingen: Vandenhoeck und Ruprecht, 1955).

Whitley, D.E.H., *The Theology of St. Paul* (Philadelphia: Fortress Press, 1972).

Wilder, Amos N., 'The Rhetoric of Ancient and Modern Apocalyptic', *Interpretation* 25 (1971), pp. 36-53.

Wilson, R. McL., *Gnosis in the New Testament* (Philadelphia: Westminster Press, 1968).

Yamauchi, Edwin, *Pre-Christian Gnosticism* (Grand Rapids: Eerdmans, 1973).

Index of Biblical (and Other Ancient) References

Index of Authors

www.ingramcontent.com/pod-product-compliance
Lightning Source LLC
Chambersburg PA
CBHW071629100426
R18120200001B/R181202PG42739CBX00001B/1